OXFORD WORLD'S CLASSICS

THE DHAMMAPADA

THE *Dhammapada*, 'sayings of dhamma'—that is, religiously inspiring statements—is the Pāli version of one of the most popular texts of the Buddhist canon. Like all religious texts in Pāli, it belongs to the Theravāda school of the Buddhist tradition whose participants are at present found primarily in Kampuchea, Laos, Myanmar, Sri Lanka, and Thailand. Compiled in verse, it is a religious work meant to inculcate a certain set of religious and ethical values, as well as a certain manner of perception of life and its problems and their solutions. That it has performed this task with remarkable success is hardly debatable. Perhaps the best testimony for that is its enduring popularity among Buddhists of all denominations, throughout the centuries of their existence.

JOHN ROSS CARTER is Professor and Chair of the Department of Philosophy and Religion and the Robert Hung Ngai Ho Professor of Asian Studies at Colgate University. He has written, edited, and contributed to several other books on the religious traditions of Asia.

MAHINDA PALIHAWADANA is Professor of Sanskrit Emeritus at Sri Jayawardhanapura University in Sri Lanka. He has written several articles on Theravāda Buddhist thought.

OXFORD WORLD'S CLASSICS

*For over 100 years Oxford World's Classics have brought
readers closer to the world's great literature. Now with over 700
titles—from the 4,000-year-old myths of Mesopotamia to the
twentieth century's greatest novels—the series makes available
lesser-known as well as celebrated writing.*

*The pocket-sized hardbacks of the early years contained
introductions by Virginia Woolf, T. S. Eliot, Graham Greene,
and other literary figures which enriched the experience of reading.
Today the series is recognized for its fine scholarship and
reliability in texts that span world literature, drama and poetry,
religion, philosophy and politics. Each edition includes perceptive
commentary and essential background information to meet the
changing needs of readers.*

OXFORD WORLD'S CLASSICS

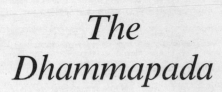

The Dhammapada

Translated with an Introduction and Notes by
JOHN ROSS CARTER
and
MAHINDA PALIHAWADANA

OXFORD
UNIVERSITY PRESS

OXFORD
UNIVERSITY PRESS

Great Clarendon Street, Oxford OX2 6DP

Oxford University Press is a department of the University of Oxford.
It furthers the University's objective of excellence in research, scholarship,
and education by publishing worldwide in

Oxford New York

Athens Auckland Bangkok Bogotá Buenos Aires Calcutta
Cape Town Chennai Dar es Salaam Delhi Florence Hong Kong Istanbul
Karachi Kuala Lumpur Madrid Melbourne Mexico City Mumbai
Nairobi Paris São Paulo Singapore Taipei Tokyo Toronto Warsaw

with associated companies in Berlin Ibadan

Published in the United States
by Oxford University Press Inc., New York

British Library Cataloguing in Publication Data

Data available

Library of Congress Cataloging in Publication Data

Tipitaka. Suttapitaka. Khuddakanikaya. Dhammapada English.
The Dhammapada / translated with an introduction and notes by
John Ross Carter and Mahinda Palihawadana.
(Oxford world's classics)
I. Carter, John Ross. II. Palihawadana, Mahinda. III. Title. IV. Series.
BQ1372.E54 C36 2000 294.3′82322—dc21 00–037519
ISBN 0–19–283613–7

4

Typeset in Times
by RefineCatch Limited, Bungay, Suffolk
Printed in Great Britain by
Clays Ltd, St Ives plc

To
Kusuma and Sandra
and for
Priyamvada, Ravindra, Nirmala, Ruchira,
Christopher John, Mary Elizabeth

PREFACE

Twenty-two years ago our project of translating the *Dhammapada* was launched when we began work together in Sri Lanka. Over the years our long-distance correspondence has witnessed enormous change: from a time when it took more than one month to receive a response by one of us to the other's work on one segment of the project, to today's email, when a reply is often received in the same day. Our larger work, *The Dhammapada*, was first published by Oxford University Press in 1987, with a paperback edition, containing a new introduction, appearing in 1998. It was a massive undertaking. In that work, we decided to provide first a new English translation of the Pāli verses followed by a presentation of the Pāli text together with the English translation both of the verses and of the commentarial glosses on words appearing in those verses. We followed the order of presentation of the verses developed by the fifth-century Pāli commentary on the *Dhammapada* (the *Dhammapadaṭṭhakathā*). We decided not to stop there. We continued searching later Sinhala commentarial sources running from the tenth to the twentieth century to provide, in extensive notes, our own critical textual comments as well as translations of elaborations on doctrinal matters. And throughout that work we integrated scholarly discussions available at the time of issues dealing with the early and received text.

That earlier and larger work, from which the English translation of the verses appears here with but very few changes, remains available for anyone wishing to pursue in greater depth issues that might arise from reading the verses appearing in this volume in the Oxford World's Classics series. We have designed this present translation of the most popular canonical text among Buddhists, and one of the great religious texts of the world, for the general reader, and notes have been included to provide some elaboration of terms and concepts that might not be entirely clear at first reading.

J.R.C.
M.P.

Hamilton, NY
Maharagama

CONTENTS

INTRODUCTION

THE *Dhammapada* is among the most popular canonical texts in the Buddhist world. It is quoted by politicians, and students learn it by heart in the original Pāli in Buddhist schools in countries such as Sri Lanka. New translations of it appear in print every few years. In fact it has had a remarkable history of being translated into other languages, beginning with the oldest Chinese version called the *Fa-chü-ching*, which is known to have been done in 224 after Christ.

The *Dhammapada* that is translated in this volume is the Pāli version of a type of text which was in use among Buddhists from very ancient times. Like all religious texts in Pāli, it belongs to the Theravāda school of the Buddhist tradition whose adherents are at present found primarily in Kampuchea, Laos, Myanmar, Sri Lanka, and Thailand. The origin of the text, however, goes back to the formative days of the Theravāda school in India in the two or three centuries that followed the death of the Buddha. Some at least of the other Buddhist schools that originated in India around the same time also had their own versions of this text. Four complete or nearly complete versions are extant: (1) the Pāli *Dhammapada*; (2) the Gāndhārī *Dharmapada* in the Prakrit language of Gandhāra in the north-west of the Indian subcontinent, surmised to belong to the Dharmaguptaka school; (3) the *Dharmapada* of the Sarvāstivāda school in mixed Sanskrit, called the *Udānavarga*, and (4) the text known as the Patna *Dharmapada*, which was published for the first time in 1979 and which is in a partly Sanskritized language somewhat akin to Pāli. It has been surmised that this may be the *Dharmapada* of the Mahīśāsaka school. Quotations from a *Dharmapada* chapter in the *Mahā-vastu*, a work in mixed Sanskrit of the ancient Mahāsānghika Lokottaravāda school, provide evidence of a fifth version.

The title *Dhammapada* means 'sayings of dhamma' (or dharma if we use the Sanskrit form of the word). Dhamma/dharma signifies specifically 'the Buddha's teaching', but more generally also 'religious truth' or what morally uplifts and sustains the person who lives according to it. The title therefore implies that the text contains religiously inspiring statements made by the Buddha on various occasions. They are all in verse. A considerable number of them are also found in other works of the Buddhist canon. Moreover, equivalents of a few of these verses are also found, with varying degrees of difference, among old Indian aphoristic verses in such works as the epic *Mahābhārata*.

How could such a text, with several versions in different ancient Buddhist languages and verses whose counterparts are found in non-Buddhist Indian works, have originated among the Buddhists in the first place? It would have been easy to answer this question if we could say that one of them is the original *Dhammapada* and the others are translations of it into the different languages that the early Buddhists used. Unfortunately it is not as easy as that, although some used to think that the Pāli text was the original *Dhammapada*. These texts, though undoubtedly of one genre, are also considerably different from one another. They differ in size and arrangement, and frequently in the wording of individual stanzas as well. Let us take size, for example. While the Pāli text has 423 stanzas, the Patna *Dharmapada* (of which only a single manuscript has survived) indicates that it originally consisted of 502 stanzas, although the extant manuscript has only 414. The *Udānavarga* with more than 1,000 stanzas is the longest. The Gāndhārī *Dharmapada*, about 40 per cent of which is missing in the only available manuscript on which the printed editions are based, is estimated to have had about 540 stanzas.

It is the same with arrangement. All texts of this genre agree in distributing the verses they contain in a number of chapters or 'groups' (*vagga* in Pāli, *varga* in Sanskrit). For these chapter headings, the different *Dharmapada*s often use the same titles, or synonymous titles (and also a few that are specific to each version), but the verses that appear under the same or similar titles are not identical in the different versions. There are some common verses under a common chapter heading, but the number of such verses among the different versions is disproportionate.

A considerable number of the individual stanzas can be regarded as nearly 'identical,' if we disregard the linguistic differences that are naturally to be expected in these compilations (which are, after all, in different though closely related dialects or languages). More often, however, they are not quite identical, but, rather, contain a variant word or phrase or line (behind which a text critic might on occasion find quite a treasure trove!). But, as the numbers mentioned above would indicate, there are also, apart from these 'identical' and similar verses, a varying number of stanzas exclusive to each version of this genre of texts. One must hasten to add, however, that, even in this exclusivity, there is a similarity that should not be overlooked. A verse may be found in one *Dharmapada* that is not found in another; as a *dharma* saying, it could have been just as eligible for inclusion in any of these texts, but it was not the preference of a particular compiler or compilers to include that verse in the text concerned.

In the end, the question of how this kind of text originated and proliferated is paired with the question of how the Buddhist canonical texts came into existence, how the Buddhist sects or schools evolved, and what the languages were that the different schools used.

It would appear that even during the Buddha's lifetime there were monks who were able to recount from memory the contents of his discourses which they had either heard directly or had learned from reports that circulated among his disciples. There is evidence to show that the gist of some important discourses had even been turned into verse and memorized in that form.

Soon after the death of the Buddha it appears that leading members of the community of monks set to work on compiling an authoritative corpus of discourses relating to his teaching and to the discipline which he enjoined on the monks. The different schools of the Buddhist tradition have left accounts of this momentous undertaking in Buddhist history. On its main events they are in broad agreement, though they differ over details. This activity started with the summoning of an assembly of the most respected members of the Saṅgha (the community of monks) at Rājagaha, capital city of the kingdom of Magadha. At this assembly, generally referred to as the First Council, it was decided that Ānanda, who as the Buddha's personal attendant had the widest knowledge of the events of the Teacher's life, should rehearse the contents of his speeches and conversations as he remembered them, with some description of the circumstances associated with each such discourse. Ānanda's long report, constituting a narration of the many separate events, was formally endorsed by the assembled monks, and by common consent it was later named the *Sutta Piṭaka* ('Basket' of Discourses), which in turn was subdivided into a number of 'collections'. A similar report, dealing with matters connected with the promulgation of the code of discipline (*Vinaya*) which was to be followed by the Saṅgha, was made by the monk Upāli and was accepted by the assembly, later to be designated the *Vinaya Piṭaka* (the 'Basket' of the Discipline). There is no evidence of the adoption of a third similar compilation at this assembly, but the Buddhist tradition as a whole acknowledges the existence of a third 'Basket' known as the *Abhidhamma Piṭaka*. It probably developed in later times by a process of systematization and elaboration of certain lists of principles which seem to have been mentioned at this rehearsal. The Basket of Discourses was subdivided into a number of 'collections.' Among them was the Minor Collection (*Khuddaka-nikāya*) which consisted of a number of separate works. Whether this collection dates back to the original rehearsal is not altogether certain, because several of the ancient schools mention it as a canonical text while several others do not. Many works of the Minor Collection are characterized by comparative brevity; a number of them also happen to be among the most popular works of the Buddhist canon. An interesting notice in a later Pāli commentary on one of these works—the *Itivuttaka*— informs us that its contents were in the first instance memorized by a slave girl who heard the Buddha teaching them to the monks. It was the 'recovery' of those teachings through her (she had become a lay devotee of the Buddha) that led to them being rehearsed at the First Council. This may be taken as an indication of the nature of the Minor Collection and of the reason why there was no unanimity of opinion on the suitability of these works to be reckoned as part of the canon. The *Dhammapada* finds its place in the canon as one of the works of the Minor Collection. Since many of its verses are also found elsewhere in the canon, the unavoidable conclusion is that it cannot be regarded as a report of a discourse or even of several discourses, in the same sense as some of the other works of the canon can be so described. Rather, it consists for the most part of metrical portions that had been taken over from various discourses; for that reason it has an anthological character. But it was accorded canonical status, and it cannot be regarded as merely an anthology.

With our present knowledge, we can say that a compilation of *dharma* verses appears to have been in existence from very early times—almost certainly from before the formation of separate schools—and this was considered as part of the Buddhist canon. However, we cannot speak of a definite 'text' which was the 'original *Dharmapada*'. What is more likely is that what were called *dharmupadāni* or dharma verses when referring to works of the Minor Collection may have been something more fluid than a 'text'. They might rather have constituted a 'quasi-text', open-ended as it were, which allowed the various schools to restructure them considerably and add more verses taken from other acceptable sources. (Many other works adopted at the First Council also seem to have remained more or less as such quasi-texts, which were subjected to certain changes in the different schools, until they were 'fixed' by being turned into written works about the beginning of the Christian era.) The extant *Dhammapada* of the Theravāda school contains several verses which on good grounds can be deemed to have been added to an originally shorter text.

Judging from the number of common verses in the extant texts of this genre, we can surmise that this early 'quasi-text', which came to be regarded as an essential part of the sacred works of several Buddhist schools, must have been considerably smaller than either of the two smallest of the extant dharma

texts—namely, the Pāli *Dhammapada* of the Theravāda school
or the Patna *Dharmapada*. It could be said that the extant
*Dharmapada*s developed from this 'quasi-text' by a process of
linguistic redaction, expansion of content, and chapter
rearrangement. Neither the basic format nor the essential nature
of the contents was affected by this process.

Regarding the process of linguistic redaction, it is a historical
fact that the most sacred works of the Buddhist tradition—its
canonical texts—are preserved in several languages. The only
complete recension to survive in an ancient Indian language is
the Pāli canon, but varyingly incomplete recensions have been
preserved in several related Indo-Aryan languages. Most of
these show signs of having been affected by a process of Sanskritization; that is, texts which were originally in some Indo-
Aryan vernaculars have been 'polished' by changing the words
as far as possible into their corresponding Sanskrit forms.

Apparently this process was a result of the re-emergence of
the prestige of the Sanskrit tradition in India with the fall of the
Mauryan Empire in the second century BC, after the setbacks it
experienced due to the efflorescence of religious movements during nearly three centuries after the time of the Buddha. The
process of Sanskritization seems to have gathered more
momentum after the hitherto orally transmitted texts were
committed to writing. Hence, the later a version of a work
assumed written form, the more Sanskritized the language tends
to be. Buddhist texts that were taken out of India before the
beginning of the Christian era appear to have escaped the more
blatant aspects of this artificial process of Sanskritization.

The Sanskritization, however, was never a complete trans-
formation, and the affected texts are full of forms which are
inadmissible in classical Sanskrit. With the help of these 'hybrid'
words, modern research has been painstakingly trying to unravel
the identities of the original languages that lie behind these
Sanskritized Buddhist texts. The evidence brought to light in
this way shows that the Buddhist canonical texts were originally
compiled and preserved in several languages, possibly four or
more.

The extant *Dhammapada* recensions reflect this situation perfectly. The Pāli *Dhammapada* would have naturally been brought to Sri Lanka in the third century BC with the official introduction of the Theravāda tradition to the island (said to have been the work of missionaries sent by Emperor Aśoka), or shortly thereafter along with the other sacred texts of the tradition. (It is not quite correct to say that 'texts' were brought. It was not customary to commit sacred works to writing; they were preserved only in the memory of those who dedicated themselves to their study. In a sense, therefore, the texts were not physically apart from the missionaries themselves.) The result was that the Pāli *Dhammapada*, along with other Theravāda canonical works, escaped much of the Sanskritic influence to which texts of the Indian schools were subjected; they were preserved largely in the linguistic form which had evolved by about the third century BC among the adherents of Theravāda for purposes of their religious activities. (It must be stated, however, that even in the evolution of that linguistic form Sanskrit seems to have been a major influence.)

When the Theravāda canon was committed to writing in Sri Lanka about the beginning of the Christian era, it put a halt to any further large-scale modifications of the texts. But a close examination of the material of the *Dhammapada* reveals that at some earlier stage, parts of it had been considerably different in form, and they had been modified to conform to the characteristics which are normative of the language of the Theravāda canon. (This is also true of the other canonical texts.) According to the Theravāda tradition, this language is Māgadhī, that is, the language of Magadha, the region of ancient India in which the Buddha for the most part conducted his mission. Modern scholarship generally discounts this view.

As for the Gāndhārī *Dharmapada*, its text was recovered thanks to the fact that two French travellers, MM. Dutreuil de Rhins and Grenard, and a Russian diplomat, N. Th. Petrovskii, independently acquired in 1892 two parts of a very ancient birch-bark manuscript written in the Kharoṣṭhī script, which according to reports was discovered in the valley of the Karakāsh river, 21 kilometres from Khotan. (A third portion of this priceless document, which seems to have been withheld by the persons who sold it, has not yet been recovered.) The manuscript, dated to the first or second century after Christ, is one of the oldest discovered in the Indian subcontinent. At this time, and in this remote part of the land, the process of Sanskritization had obviously not yet advanced very far; therefore, the text of this *Dharmapada* is preserved in a linguistic form which is still a Prakrit—a 'vernacular' language—and in this instance Gāndhārī, the language of Gandhāra.The Patna *Dharmapada* was discovered by Rāhula Sāṅkṛtyāyana among Indian manuscripts in Tibet in 1934. The work has been printed based on photographs of this single manuscript, which has been dated in the second half of the twelfth century. The language of the work is a Sanskritized Prakrit, but some of the word forms found in it preserve features that are more archaic than their correspondents in the Pāli text.

The *Udānavarga* is a *Dharmapada* text that modern scholarship has recovered from numerous fragmentary manuscript remains discovered in East Turkestan, where it was obviously a phenomenally popular work. A unique fact about this *Dharmapada* is that its Chinese translator of the fourth century, as well as a well-known Sanskrit *Abhidharma* commentator, Yaśomitra, of the eighth century, ascribed its compilation to a particular individual called Dharmatrāta, a celebrated doctor of the Sarvāstivāda school, who lived in the first century after Christ. The *Abhidharma* commentator says that Dharmatrāta extracted various dharma verses from the Basket of Discourses and arranged them in chapters and produced the *Udāna*. This is now not taken as literally true, but as an indication that a scholar of the first century put the finishing touches to the *Dharmapada* text of his particular school, the Sarvāstivāda, and fixed it in a definite form. The manuscript remains of this text stem from a variety of periods; one of the striking features that emerge from them is that readings of the earlier documents reveal a text that is less Sanskritized than the vulgate, which is based on the later manuscripts. The vulgate is so Sanskritized that it is often referred to as the Sanskrit *Dharmapada*.

From the foregoing, it should become clear that the reason why we have so many *Dharmapada* texts is that the different

Buddhist schools that came into being in the course of the tradition's history used their own specific linguistic format to transmit the sacred texts, including this particular text. Whether the texts of the different schools were redacted or translated from a single corpus in an 'original language' of the Buddhist tradition is a vexing question to which no clear answer can be given. What has become clear from years of research is that none of the existing traditions can claim that its religious language is the language of the Buddha or the language in which the First Council was conducted. Whatever was the language of the First Council, it seems likely that Buddhists in the various localities of India transmitted the discourses that were accepted as genuine at the Council in their local languages. When schisms took place and sects or schools arose, each sect must necessarily have had a local centre that eventually became its 'headquarters'. It is reasonable to assume that the language of that locality would have become the language of the school. But, in this role, the particular language seems to have been subjected to a process of 'polishing', in the course of which it must have lost a considerable part of its original vernacular character. This is why it is difficult to regard any of the existing text-collections as representative of the earliest language of the Buddhist tradition.

Although the *Dharmapada* texts of the different schools varied in language, size, and chapter arrangement, there were hardly any differences among them when it came to contents. Since the *Dharmapada*s (plural) were selections of verses from the discourses (and other such sources) that were made by monks of the early schools for the obvious purpose of advising Buddhists on how to lead the good life (to take dharma to the people), we should expect their contents to be somewhat circumscribed by that particular social requirement. That is probably why their different versions do not reflect any of the abstruse differences that characterize the various Buddhist schools. Instead, they reflect the basics of the teaching and what in it was thought to be most relevant to the day-to-day life of the people.

The work advises, explicitly and implicitly, that one must engage oneself in the process of learning dhamma. It asks,

> Who shall conquer this earth and the realm of Yama,
> This [human realm] together with [the realm of] gods?
> Who shall pluck a well-taught dhamma word
> Like an expert, a flower?

and goes on to answer,

> A learner shall conquer this earth and the realm of Yama,
> This [human realm] together with [the realm of] gods.
> A learner shall pluck a well-taught dhamma word
> Like an expert, a flower. (vv. 44–5)

Learning dhamma, one learns to steady the mind:

> The quivering, wavering mind,
> Hard to guard, hard to check,
> The sagacious one makes straight,
> Like a fletcher, an arrow shaft. (v. 33)

There is no disaster worse than the mind that is not tended.

> What a foe may do to a foe,
> Or a hater to a hater—
> Far worse than that
> The mind ill held may do to him. (v. 42)

The secret of the mind 'well held' is meditative awareness and restraint:

> By standing alert, by awareness,
> By restraint and control too,
> The intelligent one could make an island
> That a flood does not overwhelm. (v. 25)

But whether one rightly tends one's mind, or does the opposite, is solely dependent on what one does oneself:

> By oneself is wrong done,
> By oneself is one defiled.
> By oneself wrong is not done,
> By oneself, surely, is one cleansed.
> One cannot purify another;
> Purity and impurity are in oneself [alone]. (v. 165)

> Oneself indeed is patron of oneself.
> Who else indeed could be one's patron?
> With oneself well restrained,
> One gets a patron hard to get. (v. 160)

One must not forget that one reaps the consequence of one's action. It may take time, but it will surely come:

> For a bad act done does not coagulate
> Like freshly extracted milk.
> Burning, it follows the childish one,
> Like fire concealed in ashes. (v 71)

> Think not triflingly of wrong,
> 'It will not come to me!'
> With falling drops of water,
> Even a waterpot is filled.
> A childish one is filled with wrong,
> Acquiring bit by bit. (v. 121)

One must concede to others what one wishes for oneself. In this way one must learn to respect life and be sensitive to the rights of others:

> All are frightened of the rod.
> Of death all are afraid.
> Having made oneself the example,
> One should neither slay nor cause to slay. (v. 129)

To become a source of peace, one must learn to get out of the spiral of harbouring grudges and retaliation:

> 'He reviled me! He struck me!
> He defeated me! He robbed me!'
> They who gird themselves up with this,
> For them enmity is not quelled. (v. 3)

> Not by enmity are enmities quelled,
> Whatever the occasion here.
> By the absence of enmity are they quelled.
> This is an ancient truth. (v. 5)

The *Dhammapada* is full of such simple advice. However, it also rather unexpectedly plunges into more profound levels of the

Buddhist teachings. Nothing illustrates this better than the
opening verses of the text itself:

> Preceded by perception are mental states,
> For them is perception supreme,
> From perception have they sprung.
> If, with perception polluted, one speaks or acts,
> Thence suffering follows
> As a wheel the draught ox's foot. (v. 1)

Or consider the following which combines the simple with the
complex in fascinating style:

> In the sky there is no footstep;
> The recluse is not in externals;
> Enamoured with preoccupying tendencies are the generations;
> Free of preoccupying tendencies are Tathāgatas. (v. 254)

The *Dhammapada* sometimes strikes a critical note and con-
trasts some current teaching or practice with what ought to be
the better practice, that is, the Buddhist practice,

> Many for refuge go
> To mountains and to forests . . .
> Humans who are threatened by fear . . .
>
> This is not a refuge secure . . .
>
> But who to the Buddha, Dhamma,
> And Saṅgha as refuge has gone,
> Sees with full insight
> The Four Noble Truths . . .
>
> This, indeed, is a refuge secure. (vv. 188–92, abridged)

and proclaims the virtues of the Buddhist 'path' in typically
Buddhist terms:

> Of paths, the eightfold is the best.
> Of truths, the four statements. . . .
>
> Just this path, there is no other
> For purity of vision. . . .
>
> By you is the task strenuously to be done;
> Tathāgatas are proclaimers. . . .
>
> When through wisdom one perceives,
> 'All *saṃkhāras* are transient,' . . .

'All *saṃkhāras* are suffering,' . . .

'All dhammas are without self,'
Then one is detached as to misery.
This is the path of purity. (vv. 273–4, 276–9, abridged)

At times the text reads like words of critical advice meant solely for the Buddhist monk, though such instances are not numerous:

He would desire unreal glory
And pre-eminence among bhikkhus,
Authority, too, concerning dwellings,
And offerings in other families. (v. 73)

The means of acquisition is one,
And another the way leading to Nibbāna.
Having recognized this as so,
Let a bhikkhu who is a disciple of the Buddha
Not delight in [receiving] esteem;
Let him cherish disengagement. (v. 75)

At some places in the text one comes across a saying that sounds puzzling, or out of tune with what one would expect to be Theravāda teachings:

Who has no faith, the ungrateful one,
The man who is a burglar,
Who has destroyed opportunities, ejected wish,
Truly he is a person supreme. (v. 97)

But this is neither irony nor paradox, but simply a ticklish statement which is meant to be correctly interpreted—a task the Commentary gladly undertakes.[1] But look at this:

If on the hand a wound were not,
One could carry poison with [that] hand.
Poison does not follow one without a wound.
No wrong there is for one not doing it. (v. 124)

---

[1] See the gloss provided below on this verse. The Commentary on the *Dhammapada* (*Dhammapadaṭṭhakathā*) consulted in this translation appears itself to have been translated from old Sinhala comments into the Pāli language in Sri Lanka in the fifth century after Christ. The translator of the Commentary remains unknown.

The Commentary brings this into line with the traditional teaching by interpreting the word 'doing' as meaning 'intentionally committing'—which is not very convincing. The verse remains a puzzle and reminds one more of the *Bhagavad Gītā* teaching of 'detached action'.

Just as unusual from a strictly Theravāda point of view is the following:

> Just so, one who has done wholesome deeds
> Has gone from this world to the beyond —
> The wholesome deeds receive such a one,
> Like relatives, a dear one who has returned. (v. 220)

This spatial detachment of deeds from the doer seems to fit better in the theoretical structure underpinning Brahmanical sacrificial practices than in Buddhist thought. Not quite in agreement with early Buddhist teaching on karma is this stanza:

> That spot in the world is not found
> Neither in the sky nor in the ocean's depths,
> Nor having entered into a cleft in mountains,
> Where abiding, one would be released from the bad deed. (v. 127)

This almost borders on fatalism and is to that degree contradictory to stanzas 172–3 of this compilation.

Although the *Dhammapada* is essentially based on the teachings of the Buddhist heritage, yet not only Buddhists but most religious people would agree with much that is said in this collection, even where it may be in words that sound characteristically Buddhist. Consider, for example, the following:

> When a need has arisen, friends are a blessing,
> A blessing is contentment with whatever [there be],
> A blessing is the wholesome deed at the end of life,
> A blessing it is to relinquish all sorrow.

> A blessing in the world is reverence for mother,
> A blessing, too, is reverence for father . . .

> A blessing is virtue into old age,
> A blessing is faith established,
> A blessing is the attainment of insight-wisdom,
> A blessing it is to refrain from doing wrongs. (vv. 331–3 abridged)

Or consider, further, a well-known verse:

> Refraining from all that is detrimental,
> The attainment of what is wholesome,
> The purification of one's mind:
> This is the instruction of Awakened Ones. (v. 183)

And on occasion a verse in the collection is simply an Indian aphorism, found also in comparable terms in Hindu texts, as in the following:

> For one in the habit of showing respect,
> Of always honouring elder ones,
> Four qualities increase:
> Life, complexion, ease, and strength. (v. 109)

But not all that is found in the *Dhammapada* is religious teaching in the strict sense. Some stanzas are couched in words that sound autobiographical. Consider the following:

> Like an elephant in battle,
> The arrow shot from a bow,
> I shall endure the unwarranted word;
> The majority, indeed, are of poor virtue. (v. 320)

Or the following:

> I ran through *samsāra*, with its many births,
> Searching for, but not finding, the house-builder.
> Misery is birth again and again.
>
> House-builder, you are seen!
> The house you shall not build again!
> Broken are your rafters, all,
> Your roof beam destroyed.
> Freedom from *samkhāras* has the mind attained.
> To the end of cravings has it come. (vv. 153–4)

It has been remarked that though here and there among the verses of the *Dhammapada* we find some fragments of excellent poetry, what we have in it in general are 'accumulations of insipid mediocrity which piety preserves'.[2] Though this may be

---

[2] So John Brough in his 'Preface' to *The Gāndhārī Dharmapada*, edited with an introduction and commentary by John Brough (London: Oxford University Press, 1962), p. xvii. His complete sentence reads: 'The resulting vast accumulations of insipid mediocrity which piety preserves are by no means peculiar to Buddhism.'

a harsh judgement, there is much truth in it. For example, who can refrain from asking what poetry is there in the following?

> Who with a rod harms the offenceless, the harmless,
> To one of ten places quite quickly one goes down:

> Harshly painful feelings, destitution, and fracturing of the body,
> Grave illness too, even disarrayed mind, one would attain,

> Trouble from the king or severe slander,
> Even loss of relatives or dissolution of possessions,

> And also fire, the purifier, burns his houses.
> And upon the breaking of his body, the unwise one falls into
>   hell. (vv. 137–40)

The important point, however, is that the *Dhammapada* was not compiled as poetry and one should not look for poetry in it. It is a religious work, meant to inculcate a certain set of religious and ethical values and a certain manner of perception of life and its problems and their solutions. That it has performed this task with remarkable success is hardly debatable. Perhaps the best testimony for that is its enduring popularity among Buddhists of all denominations, throughout the centuries of their existence.

SELECT BIBLIOGRAPHY

General Background

Adikaram, E. W., *Early History of Buddhism in Ceylon* (Colombo: M. D. Gunasena, 1953; 1st pub. 1946).

Horner, I. B., 'Buddhism: The Theravada', in R. C. Zaehner (ed.), *Concise Encyclopaedia of Living Faiths* (Boston: Beacon Press, 1967; 1st pub. 1959).

Ñāṇamoli, Bhikkhu, *The Path of Purification* (Colombo: A. Semage, 2nd edn., 1964; 1st pub. 1956).

Nyanaponika Thera, *Satipaṭṭhāna: The Heart of Buddhist Meditation* (York Beach, Me.: Samuel Weiser, 1984; 1st pub. 1962).

Nyanatiloka, *Guide to the Abhidhamma Piṭaka: Being a Synopsis of the Philosophical Collection Belonging to the Buddhist Pali Canon* (Kandy: Buddhist Publication Society, 3rd edn., 1971).

— *Buddhist Dictionary: Manual of Buddhist Terms and Doctrines*, (3rd revised and enlarged edn. ed. Nyanaponika (Colombo: Frewin & Co., 1972; 1st pub. 1952).

Rahula, Walpola Sri, *What the Buddha Taught* (rev. edn., New York: Grove Press, 1974; 1st pub. 1959).

Upasak, C. S., *Dictionary of Early Buddhist Monastic Terms (Based on Pali Literature)* (Varanasi: Bharati Prakashan, 1975).

Vajirañāṇa Mahāthera, Paravahera, *Buddhist Meditation in Theory and Practice: A General Exposition According to the Pali Canon of the Theravada School* (Colombo: M. D. Gunasena & Co., 1962).

Dhammapada Translations

Carter, John Ross, and Palihawadana, Mahinda, *The Dhammapada: A New English Translation with the Pali Text and the First English Translation of the Commentary's Explanation of the Verses with Notes Translated from Sinhala Sources and Critical Textual Comments* (New York: Oxford University Press, 1987; issued as an Oxford University Press paperback, 1998).

Dhammajoti, Bhikkhu Kuala Lumpur, *The Chinese Version of the Dharmapada: Translated with Introduction and Annotations* (University of Kelaniya, Sri Lanka: Postgraduate Institute of Pali and Buddhist Studies, 1995).

Fausbøll, V., *Dhammapadam: Ex tribus codicibus hauniensibus palice edidit, latine vertit, excerptis ex commentario palico nostique illustravit* (Copenhagen: no pub., 1855; 2nd edn. (text and Latin translation only), London, 1900).

Kalupahana, David J., *A Path of Righteousness—Dhammapada: An Introductory Essay, Together with the Pali Text, English Translation and Commentary* (Lanham, Md.: University Press of America, 1986).

Max Müller, F., *The Dhammapada: A Collection of Verses, Being One of the Canonical Books of the Buddhists. Translated from Pali*, Sacred Books of the East 10, part I (Oxford: Clarendon Press, 1881).

Norman, K. R., *The Word of the Doctrine (Dhammapada)*, Pali Text Society Translation Series 46 (Oxford: published by the Pali Text Society, 1997).

Radhakrishnan, S., *The Dhammapada, with Introductory Essays, Pali Text, English Translation and Notes* (London: Oxford University Press, 2nd impression, 1954; 1st pub. 1950).

Rhys Davids, C. A. F., *The Minor Anthologies of the Pali Canon*, part i: *Dhammapada and Khuddhakapatha*, Sacred Books of the Buddhists 7 (London: Pali Text Society, 1931).

Further Reading in Oxford World's Classics

Bhagavad Gita, trans. and ed. W. J. Johnson.

Dharmasūtras, trans. and ed. Patrick Olivelle.

Santideva, *The Bodhicaryavatara*, trans. and ed. Kate Crosby and Andrew Skilton, with a general introduction by Paul Williams.

The Sauptikaparvan (from the Mahabharata), trans. William Johnson.

Upaniṣads, trans. and ed. Patrick Olivelle.

THE
DHAMMAPADA

Chapter I The Pairs

1.　　Preceded by perception are mental states,*
　　　For them is perception supreme,
　　　From perception have they sprung.
　　　If, with perception polluted,* one speaks or acts,
　　　Thence suffering follows
　　　As a wheel the draught ox's foot.

2.　　Preceded by perception are mental states,
　　　For them is perception supreme,
　　　From perception have they sprung.
　　　If, with tranquil perception, one speaks or acts,
　　　Thence ease follows
　　　As a shadow that never departs.

3.　　'He reviled me! He struck me!
　　　He defeated me! He robbed me!'
　　　They who gird themselves up with this,
　　　For them enmity is not quelled.

4.　　'He reviled me! He struck me!
　　　He defeated me! He robbed me!'
　　　They who do not gird themselves up with this,
　　　For them is enmity quelled.

5.　　Not by enmity are enmities quelled,
　　　Whatever the occasion here.
　　　By the absence of enmity are they quelled.
　　　This is an ancient truth.

6.　　Others do not realize
　　　'We here are struggling.'
　　　Those who realize this—for them
　　　Are quarrels therefore quelled.

7. Whoever dwells seeing the pleasurable, in senses
       unrestrained,
   Immoderate in food, indolent, inferior of enterprise,
   Over him, indeed, Māra* prevails,
   Like the wind over a weak tree.

8. Whoever dwells seeing the non-pleasurable, in senses
       well restrained,
   And moderate in food, faithful, resolute in enterprise,
   Over him, indeed, Māra prevails not,
   Like the wind over a rocky crag.

9. One not free of defilements,*
   Who will don a yellow robe,*
   That one, devoid of control and truth,
   Is not worthy of a yellow robe.

10. But one who, well placed in virtues,
    Would be with defilements ejected,
    Endowed with control and truth,
    That one is worthy of a yellow robe.

11. Those who consider the non-essential as the essential,
    And see the essential as the non-essential,
    They do not attain the essential,
    Being in the pastures of improper intentions.

12. Having known the essential as the essential,
    And the superficial as the superficial,
    They attain the essential
    Who are in the pastures of proper intentions.

13. As rain penetrates
    The poorly thatched dwelling,
    So passion* penetrates
    The untended mind.

14. As rain does not penetrate
    The well-thatched dwelling,
    So passion does not penetrate
    The well-tended mind.

15. Here he grieves; having passed away he grieves;
    In both places the wrongdoer grieves.
    He grieves; he is afflicted,
    Having seen the stain of his own action.

16. Here he rejoices; having passed away he rejoices.
    In both places he who has done wholesome deeds rejoices.
    He rejoices; he is delighted,
    Having seen the purity of his own action.

17. Here he is tormented; having passed away he is
    tormented.
    In both places the wrongdoer is tormented.
    He is tormented, thinking, 'I have done wrong.'
    Gone to a state of woe,* he is tormented all the more.

18. Here he rejoices; having passed away he rejoices.
    In both places he who has done wholesome deeds rejoices.
    He rejoices, thinking, 'I have done wholesome deeds.'
    Gone to a state of weal,* he rejoices all the more.

19. If one, though reciting much of texts,
    Is not a doer thereof, a heedless man;
    He, like a cowherd counting others' cows,
    Is not a partaker in the religious quest.

20. If one, though reciting little of texts,
    Lives a life in accord with dhamma,*
    Having discarded passion, ill will, and unawareness,
    Knowing full well, the mind well freed,
    He, not grasping here, neither hereafter,
    Is a partaker of the religious quest.

Chapter II Awareness

21.   The path to the Deathless* is awareness;*
        Unawareness, the path of death.
        They who are aware do not die;
        They who are unaware are as dead.

22.   Having known this distinctly,
        Those who are wise in awareness,
        Rejoice in awareness,
        Delighted in the pasture of the noble ones.*

23.   Those meditators, persevering,
        Forever firm of enterprise,
        Those steadfast ones touch Nibbāna,*
        Incomparable release from bonds.

24.   Fame increases for the one who stands alert,
        Mindful, and of pure deeds;
        Who with due consideration acts, restrained,
        Who lives dhamma, being aware.

25.   By standing alert, by awareness,
        By restraint and control too,
        The intelligent one could make an island
        That a flood does not overwhelm.

26.   People deficient in wisdom, childish ones,
        Engage in unawareness.
        But the wise one guards awareness
        Like the greatest treasure.

27.   Engage not in unawareness,
        Nor in intimacy with sensual delight.
        Meditating, the one who is aware
        Attains extensive ease.

28. When the wise one by awareness expels unawareness,
    Having ascended the palace of wisdom,
    He, free from sorrow, steadfast,
    The sorrowing folk observes, the childish,
    As one standing on a mountain
    [Observes] those standing on the ground below.

29. Among those unaware, the one aware,
    Among the sleepers, the wide-awake,
    The one with great wisdom moves on,
    As a racehorse who leaves behind a nag.

30. By awareness, Maghavan*
    To supremacy among the gods arose.
    Awareness they praise;
    Always censured is unawareness.

31. The bhikkhu* who delights in awareness,
    Who sees in unawareness the fearful,
    Goes, burning, like a fire,
    The fetter* subtle and gross.

32. The bhikkhu who delights in awareness,
    Who sees in unawareness the fearful—
    He is not liable to suffer fall;
    In Nibbāna's presence is such a one.

Chapter III The Mind

33.   The quivering, wavering mind,
    Hard to guard, hard to check,
    The sagacious one makes straight,
    Like a fletcher, an arrow shaft.

34.   Like a water creature
    Plucked from its watery home and thrown on land,
    This mind flaps;
    [Fit] to discard [is] Māra's sway.

35.   Commendable is the taming
    Of mind, which is hard to hold down,
    Nimble, alighting wherever it wants.
    Mind subdued brings ease.

36.   The sagacious one may tend the mind,
    Hard to be seen, extremely subtle,
    Alighting wherever it wants.
    The tended mind brings ease.

37.   They who will restrain the mind,
    Far-ranging, roaming alone,
    Incorporeal, lying ahiding—
    They are released from Māra's bonds.

38.   For one of unsteady mind,
    Who knows not dhamma true,
    Whose serenity is adrifting,
    Wisdom becomes not full.

39.   No fear is there for the wide-awake
    Who has mind undamped
    And thought unsmitten—
    The wholesome and the detrimental* left behind.

40.   Knowing this body as a pot of clay,
     Securing this mind as a citadel,
     One may fight Māra with wisdom's weapon,
     Guard what has been gained—and be unattached.

41.   Soon indeed
     This body on the earth will lie,
     Pitched aside, without consciousness,
     Like a useless chip of wood.

42.   What a foe may do to a foe,
     Or a hater to a hater —
     Far worse than that
     The mind ill held may do to him.

43.   Not mother, father, nor even other kinsmen,
     May do that [good to him—]
     Far better than that
     The mind well held may do to him.

Chapter IV Flowers

44. Who shall conquer this earth and the realm of Yama,*
    This [human realm] together with [the realm of] gods?
    Who shall pluck a well-taught dhamma word
    Like an expert, a flower?

45. A learner* shall conquer this earth and the realm of Yama,
    This [human realm] together with [the realm of] gods.
    A learner shall pluck a well-taught dhamma word
    Like an expert, a flower.

46. Knowing this body to be like foam,
    Awakening to its mirage nature,
    Cutting out Māra's flowers, one may go
    Beyond the sight of the King of Death.*

47. Death takes away
    The man with attached mind,
    Plucking only flowers,
    Like a great flood, a sleeping village.

48. The End-Maker* overpowers
    The man with attached mind,
    Insatiate in sensual pleasures,
    Plucking only flowers.

49. Even as a bee, having taken up nectar
    From a flower, flies away,
    Not harming its colour and fragrance,
    So may a sage wander through a village.

50. Let one regard
    Neither the discrepancies of others,
    Nor what is done or left undone by others,
    But only the things one has done oneself or left undone.

51. Just as a brilliant flower,
    Full of colour, [but] scentless,
    So is a well-spoken word fruitless
    For one who does not do it.

52. Just as a brilliant flower,
    Full of colour and fragrance,
    So is a well-spoken word fruitful
    For one who does it.

53. Just as many garland strands
    One could make from a mass of flowers,
    So, much that is wholesome ought to be done
    By a mortal born [into this world].

54. No flower's fragrance moves against the wind,
    Neither sandalwood, *tagara*, nor *mallikā*,
    But the fragrance of the good ones moves against the
        wind;
    All directions a good person pervades.

55. Among these kinds of perfume,
    Such as sandalwood, *tagara*,
    Also waterlily and *vassikī*,
    The fragrance of virtue is incomparable.

56. Slight is this fragrance—
    The *tagara* and sandalwood—
    But the fragrance of one who is virtuous
    Wafts among the gods, supreme.

57. Māra does not find the path
    Of those who have virtue abounding,
    Who are living with awareness,
    Liberated through realization.

58. Just as in a heap of rubbish
    Cast away on a roadside,
    A lotus there could bloom,
    Of sweet fragrance, pleasing the mind,

59.   So amid the wretched, blinded ordinary folk,
      Among them who have turned to rubbish,
      The disciple of the Fully Awakened One*
      Shines surpassingly with wisdom.

Chapter V The Childish

60. Long is the night for one awake,
     Long is a league to one exhausted,
     Long is *saṃsāra** to the childish ones
     Who know not dhamma true.

61. If while moving [through life], one were not to meet
     Someone better or like unto oneself,
     Then one should move firmly by oneself;
     There is no companionship in the childish.

62. A childish person becomes anxious,
     Thinking, 'Sons are mine! Wealth is mine!'
     Not even a self* is there [to call] one's own.
     Whence sons? Whence wealth?

63. A childish one who knows his childishness
     Is, for that reason, even like a wise person.
     But a childish one who thinks himself wise
     Is truly called a childish one.

64. Even though, throughout his life,
     A childish one attends on a wise person,
     He does not [thereby] perceive dhamma,
     As a ladle, the flavour of the dish.

65. Even though, for a brief moment,
     An intelligent one attends on a wise person,
     He quickly perceives dhamma,
     As the tongue, the flavour of the dish.

66. Childish ones, of little intelligence,
     Go about with a self* that is truly an enemy;
     Performing the deed that is bad,
     Which is of bitter fruit.*

67. That deed done is not good,
    Having done which, one regrets;
    The consequence of which one receives,
    Crying with tear-stained face.

68. But that deed done is good,
    Having done which, one does not regret;
    The consequence of which one receives,
    With pleasure and with joy.

69. The childish one thinks it is like honey
    While the bad [he has done] is not yet matured.
    But when the bad [he has done] is matured,*
    Then the childish one comes by suffering.

70. Month by month a childish one
    Might eat food with a *kusa* grass blade.*
    He is not worth a sixteenth part
    Of those who have understood dhamma.

71. For a bad act done does not coagulate
    Like freshly extracted milk.
    Burning, it follows the childish one,
    Like fire concealed in ashes.

72. Only for his detriment
    Does knowledge arise for the childish one.
    It ruins his good fortune,
    Causing his [very] head to fall.

73. He would desire unreal glory
    And pre-eminence among bhikkhus,
    Authority, too, concerning dwellings,
    And offerings in other families.

74. 'Let both householders and those who have gone forth*
    Think that it is my work alone;
    In whatever is to be done or not done,
    Let them be dependent on me alone!'
    Such is the thought of the childish one;
    Desire and pride increase.

75. The means of acquisition is one,
And another the way leading to Nibbāna.
Having recognized this as so,
Let a bhikkhu who is a disciple of the Buddha
Not delight in [receiving] esteem;
Let him cherish disengagement.*

Chapter VI The Sagacious

76. The one who sees one's faults,
    Who speaks reprovingly, wise,
    Whom one would see as an indicator of treasures,
    With such a sagacious person, one would associate.
    To one associating with such a person,
    The better it will be, not the worse.

77. He would counsel, instruct,
    And restrain [one] from rude behaviour.
    To the good, he is pleasant;
    To the bad is he unpleasant.

78. Let one not associate
    With low persons, bad friends.
    But let one associate
    With noble persons, worthy friends.

79. One who drinks of dhamma sleeps at ease,
    With mind calmly clear.
    In dhamma made known by noble ones,
    The wise one constantly delights.

80. Irrigators guide the water.
    Fletchers bend the arrow shaft.
    Wood the carpenters bend.
    Themselves the wise ones tame.

81. Even as a solid rock
    Does not move on account of the wind,
    So are the wise not shaken
    In the face of blame and praise.

82. Even as a deep lake
    Is very clear and undisturbed,
    So do the wise become calm,
    Having heard the words of dhamma.

83. Everywhere, indeed, good persons 'let go'.*
    The good ones do not occasion talk, hankering for
        pleasure.
    Touched now by ease and now by misery,
    The wise manifest no high and low.

84. Neither for one's own sake nor for the sake of another,
    A son* would one wish, or wealth, or kingdom.
    One would not wish one's own prosperity by un-dhammic
        means.
    Such a one would be possessed of virtue, wisdom,
        dhamma.

85. Few are they among humans,
    The people who reach the shore beyond.*
    But these other folk
    Only run along the [hither] bank.

86. But those who live according to dhamma—
    In dhamma well proclaimed—
    Those people will reach the shore beyond.
    The realm of death is hard to cross.

87. Having forsaken a shadowy dhamma,*
    The wise one would cultivate the bright,
    Having come from familiar abode to no abode
    In disengagement, hard to relish.

88. There he would wish for delight,
    Having discarded sensual desires—he who has nothing.*
    The wise one would purify himself
    Of the defilements of the mind.

89. Whose mind is fully well cultivated in the factors of
        enlightenment,*
    Who, without clinging, delight in the rejection of grasping,
    Lustrous ones, who have destroyed intoxicants,*
    They have, in [this] world, attained Nibbāna.

Chapter VII The Worthy

90. To one who has gone the distance,*
    Who is free of sorrows, freed in every respect;
    To one who has left behind all bonds,
    Fever* there exists not.

91. The mindful ones gird up [themselves].
    In no abode* do they delight.
    Like swans having left behind a pond,
    One shelter after another they leave.

92. Those for whom there is no hoarding,*
    Who have fully understood [the nature] of food,*
    And whose pasture* is freedom
    That is empty, that has no sign,*
    Their course is hard to trace
    As that of birds in the sky.

93. In whom the influxes* are fully extinct,
    Who is not attached to sustenance,*
    And whose pasture is freedom
    That is empty and signless,
    His track is hard to trace,
    As [that] of birds in the sky.

94. Whose senses have reached an even temper,
    Like horses well trained by a charioteer,
    Who has discarded self-estimation,* who is free of influxes,
    Even the gods cherish such a one.

95. Like the earth, he does not oppose.
    A firm pillar is such a one, well cultured,
    Like a lake rid of mud.
    To such a one, travels in *saṃsāra* there are not.

96. Of such a one, pacified,
    Released by proper understanding,
    Calm is the mind,
    Calm his speech and act.

97. Who has no faith,* the ungrateful* one,
    The man who is a burglar,*
    Who has destroyed opportunities,* ejected wish,*
    Truly he is a person supreme.*

98. Whether in village or in forest,
    Whether in valley or on plateau,
    Delightful is the ground
    Where Arahants* dwell.

99. Delightful are forests
    Where people do not take delight.
    [There] those without passions will delight;
    They no sensual pleasures seek.

Chapter VIII The Thousands

100. Though a thousand be the statements,
With words of no avail,
Better is a single word of welfare,
Having heard which, one is pacified.

101. Though a thousand be the verses,
With words of no avail,
Better is a single line of verse,
Having heard which, one is pacified.

102. And should one recite a hundred verses,
With words of no avail,
Better is one dhamma word,
Having heard which, one is pacified.

103. He, truly, is supreme in battle,
Who would conquer himself alone,
Rather than he who would conquer in battle
A thousand, thousand men.

104. Better, indeed, oneself conquered
[Rather than] these other folk.
Of a person who has won himself,
Who is constantly living in self-control,

105. Neither a god nor a *gandhabba*,*
Nor Māra together with Brahmā,*
Could turn the victory into defeat
Of a living being like that.

106. Month by month, with a thousand,
One might offer sacrifice* a hundred times,
And another, to one self-composed,
Might offer worship for but a second;
Truly, that worship is better
Than what was offered a hundred years.

107. And were a living being for a hundred years
     To tend a fire* in a forest,
     And were another, to one self-composed,
     To offer worship for but a second;
     Truly, that worship is better
     Than what was offered a hundred years.

108. Whatever sacrifice or offering in the world
     One seeking merit* might sacrifice for a year;
     Even all that does not 'reach a quarter'—
     Better the respectful greetings to the straight of gait.

109. For one in the habit of showing respect,
     Of always honouring elder ones,
     Four qualities increase:
     Life, complexion, ease, and strength.

110. And should one live a hundred years
     Devoid of virtue,* uncomposed;
     Better still is one day lived
     Of one possessed of virtue, a meditator.

111. And should one live a hundred years
     Devoid of insight, uncomposed;
     Better still is one day lived
     Of one possessed of insight,* a meditator.

112. And should one live a hundred years
     Indolent, of inferior enterprise;
     Better still is one day lived
     Of one initiating enterprise, firm.

113. And should one live a hundred years
     Not seeing 'the rise and demise';*
     Better still is one day lived
     Of one seeing 'the rise and demise'.

114. And should one live a hundred years
     Not seeing the immortal state;
     Better still is one day lived
     Of one who sees the immortal state.*

115.   And should one live a hundred years
                      Not seeing dhamma supreme;
                      Better still is one day lived
                      Of one seeing dhamma supreme.

Chapter IX The Wrong

116.   Be quick in goodness;
        From wrong hold back your thought.
        Indeed, of one performing the good tardily,
        The mind delights in wrong.

117.   Should a person do a wrong,
        Let him not do it again and again.
        Let him not form a desire toward it,
        A suffering is the accumulation of wrong.

118.   Should a person do some good,
        Let him do it again and again.
        Let him form a desire toward it.
        A happiness is the accumulation of good.

119.   Even a wrongdoer experiences what is good
        As long as the detrimental* has not matured.*
        But when the detrimental is matured,
        The wrongdoer then experiences the detrimental.

120.   Even the good one experiences the detrimental
        As long as the good is not matured.
        But when the good is matured,
        Then the good one experiences the good.

121.   Think not triflingly of wrong,
        'It will not come to me!'
        With falling drops of water,
        Even a waterpot is filled.
        A childish one is filled with wrong,
        Acquiring bit by bit.

122.   Think not triflingly of good,
        'It will not come to me!'
        With falling drops of water,
        Even a waterpot is filled.
        A wise one is filled with good,
        Acquiring bit by bit.

123. One would avoid wrongs,
     Like the rich merchant with small caravan*
     The fearful road;
     Like one who loves life, poison.

124. If on the hand a wound were not,
     One could carry poison with [that] hand.
     Poison does not follow one without a wound.
     No wrong there is for one not doing it.*

125. Whoever offends an inoffensive man,
     A pure person without blemish,
     The wrong recoils on just that childish one,
     Like fine dust hurled against the wind.

126. Some are born in a womb,
     Wrongdoers, in hell.
     Those of good course go to heaven,
     To Nibbāna those without influxes.

127. That spot in the world is not found,
     Neither in the sky nor in the ocean's depths,
     Nor having entered into a cleft in mountains,
     Where abiding, one would be released from the bad
        deed.

128. That spot one does not find,
     Neither in the sky nor in the ocean's depths,
     Nor having entered into a cleft in mountains,
     Where abiding, death would not overwhelm one.*

Chapter X The Rod

129.   All are frightened of the rod.
        Of death all are afraid.
        Having made oneself the example,
        One should neither slay nor cause to slay.

130.   All are frightened of the rod.
        For all, life is dear.
        Having made oneself the example,
        One should neither slay nor cause to slay.

131.   Who with a rod does hurt
        Beings who desire ease,
        While himself looking for ease—
        He, having departed, ease does not get.

132.   Who with a rod does not hurt
        Beings who desire ease,
        While himself looking for ease—
        Having departed, ease he will get.

133.   To none speak harshly.
        Those thus addressed would retort to you.
        Miserable indeed is contentious talk.
        Retaliatory rods would touch you.

134.   If, like a flattened out metal pot,
        You yourself do not move,
        Why, Nibbāna you have attained!
        No contention is found in you.

135.   As with a rod a cowherd
        To the pasture goads his cows,
        So does old age and death
        Goad the life of living beings.

136. The childish one knows it not,
     Even while doing bad deeds.
     The one deficient in wisdom, by his own deeds
     Suffers like one burnt by fire.

137. Who with a rod harms the offenceless, the harmless,
     To one of ten places quite quickly one goes down:

138. [1] Harshly painful feelings, [2] destitution, and [3]
          fracturing of the body,
     [4] Grave illness too, [5] even disarrayed mind, one would
          attain,

139. [6] Trouble from the king or [7] severe slander,
     [8] Even loss of relatives or [9] dissolution of possessions,

140. And also [10] fire, the purifier, burns his houses.
     And upon the breaking of his body, the unwise one falls
          into hell.

141. Neither wandering about naked,* nor matted hair,* nor
          mud,
     Neither fasting, nor sleeping on hard ground,
     Nor dust and dirt, nor austere acts in the crouching
          posture,
     Cleanses a mortal who has not transcended doubts.

142. Though well adorned, if one would move with
          tranquillity,
     At peace, restrained, assured, living the higher life,
     Having put down the rod toward all beings,
     He is a *brāhmaṇa,** he, a recluse, he, a bhikkhu.

143. [Rarely] in the world is found
     A person restrained by shame,
     Who awakens to insult
     As a good horse to the whip.

144. Like a good horse struck by a whip,
     Be ardent and deeply moved.
     With faith and virtue and enterprise,
     With concentration and dhamma-discernment,
     With understanding and conduct endowed, mindful,
     You will leave behind this weighty misery.

145. Irrigators guide the water,
     Fletchers bend the arrow shaft,
     Wood the carpenters bend;
     Themselves the amenable ones* tame.

Chapter XI Old Age

146.   Oh, what laughter and why joy,
        When constantly aflame?
        In darkness enveloped,
        You do not seek the lamp.

147.   Oh, see this beautified image;*
        A mass of sores erected.
        Full of illness, highly fancied,
        Permanence it has not—or constancy.

148.   Quite wasted away is this form,
        A nest for disease, perishable.
        This putrid accumulation breaks up.
        For life has its end in death.

149.   Like these gourds
        Discarded in autumn,*
        Are grey-hued bones.
        Having seen them, what delight?

150.   Of bones the city* is made,
        Plastered with flesh and blood,
        Where decay and death are deposited,
        And pride and ingratitude.

151.   Even well-decked royal chariots wear away;
        And the body too falls into decay.
        But the dhamma of the good ones goes not to decay,
        For the good speak [of it] with the good.

152.   This unlearned person
        Grows up like an ox.
        His bulk increases,
        His wisdom increases not.

153.   I ran through *saṃsāra*, with its many births,
       Searching for, but not finding, the house-builder.
       Misery is birth again and again.

154.   House-builder, you are seen!
       The house you shall not build again!
       Broken are your rafters, all,
       Your roof beam destroyed.
       Freedom from the *saṃkhāras** has the mind attained.
       To the end of cravings has it come.*

155.   Not having lived the higher life,
       Nor having acquired wealth in youth,
       They wither away like old herons
       In a lake without fish.

156.   Not having lived the higher life,
       Nor having acquired wealth in youth,
       Like [arrows] discharged from a bow they lie
       Brooding over the things of yore.

Chapter XII The Self

157. If one would regard oneself as dear,
One would guard oneself with diligence.
The wise one would look after [himself]
During any one of the [night's] three watches.*

158. First, one would get oneself
Established in what is proper;
Then one would advise another.
[Thus] the wise one would not suffer.

159. One would oneself so do
As one advises another.
Then it is the restrained one who would restrain.
For, truly, it is the self that is hard to restrain.

160. Oneself indeed is patron of oneself.
Who else indeed could be one's patron?
With oneself well restrained,
One gets a patron hard to get.

161. The wrong done by oneself
Is born of oneself, is produced in oneself.
It grinds one deficient in wisdom
As a diamond grinds a rock-gem.

162. Whose extreme unvirtue overspreads [him],
Like the *māluvā* creeper* a *sāla* tree,
He does to himself,
Just as a foe wishes [to do] to him.

163. Easy to do are things not good
And those harmful for oneself.
But what is beneficial and good,
Is exceedingly difficult to do.

164. Who is deficient in wisdom,
     Because of detrimental view,*
     Obstructs the instruction of the Arahants,
     The Noble Ones who live dhamma;
     For one's own destruction one ripens,
     Like the fruits of a reed.*

165. By oneself is wrong done,
     By oneself is one defiled.
     By oneself wrong is not done,
     By oneself, surely, is one cleansed.
     One cannot purify another;
     Purity and impurity are in oneself [alone].

166. One would not abandon one's own purpose
     Because of the purpose of another, even though great,
     Having well understood one's own purpose,
     One would be intent on the true purpose.

Chapter XIII The World

167. To lowly quality one should not resort;
     With heedlessness one should not live.
     To an improper view one should not resort.
     And one should not be a 'world-augmenter'.*

168. One should stand up, not be neglectful,
     Follow dhamma, which is good conduct.
     One who lives dhamma sleeps at ease
     In this world and also in the next.

169. One should follow dhamma, which is good conduct,
     Not that which is poor conduct.
     One who lives dhamma sleeps at ease
     In this world and also in the next.

170. As upon a bubble one would look,
     As one would look upon a mirage,
     The one considering the world thus,
     King Death does not see.

171. Come ye, look at this world—
     Like an adorned royal chariot—
     Wherein childish ones are immersed;
     No clinging there is among those who really know.

172. And who having been heedless formerly
     But later is heedless not,
     He this world illumines
     Like the moon set free from a cloud.

173. Whose bad deed done
     Is covered by what is wholesome,
     He this world illumines
     Like the moon set free from a cloud.

174. This world has become blinded, as it were.
Few here see insightfully.
Like a bird set free from a net,
Few to heaven go.

175. Swans go along the path of the sun
And in the air they go with psychic power.*
The wise ones are led from the world,
Having conquered Māra and his cohorts.

176. Of a person who has overstepped one dhamma,*
Who speaks falsehood,
Who has turned the back on the world beyond—
There is no wrong that cannot be done.

177. Truly, no misers get to the world of gods.
Certainly, childish ones do not applaud giving.
The wise one gladly approves giving;
Hence indeed is he at ease in the hereafter.

178. Better than sole sovereignty over the earth,
Or the journey to heaven,
Than lordship over all the worlds,
Is the Fruit of Stream Attainment.*

Chapter XIV The Awakened One

179. Whose victory is not turned into defeat,
Whose victory no one in this world reaches,
That Awakened One whose range is limitless,
Him, the trackless, by what track will you lead?

180. For whom craving there is not, the netlike, the clinging,
To lead him wheresoever,
That Awakened One whose range is limitless,
Him, the trackless, by what track will you lead?

181. Those who are intent on meditating, the wise ones,
Delighting in the calm of going out,
Even gods long for them,
The Fully Enlightened Ones, the mindful.

182. Difficult is the attainment of the human state.
Difficult the life of mortals.
Difficult is the hearing of dhamma true.
Difficult the appearance of Awakened Ones.

183. Refraining from all that is detrimental,
The attainment of what is wholesome,
The purification of one's mind:
This is the instruction of Awakened Ones.

184. Forbearing patience is the highest austerity;
Nibbāna is supreme, the Awakened Ones say.
One who has gone forth is not one who hurts another,
No harasser of others is a recluse.

185. No faultfinding, no hurting, restraint in the *pātimokkha,* *
Knowing the measure regarding food, solitary bed and
   chair,
Application, too, of higher perception:
This is the instruction of the Awakened Ones.

186. Not even with a rain of golden coins
Is contentment found among sensual pleasures.
'Sensual pleasures are of little delight, are a misery.'
Knowing so, the wise one

187. Takes no delight
Even for heavenly sensual pleasures.
One who delights in the ending of craving
Is a disciple of the Fully Enlightened One.

188. Many for refuge go
To mountains and to forests,
To shrines that are groves or trees—
Humans who are threatened by fear.

189. This is not a refuge secure,
This refuge is not the highest.
Having come to this refuge,
One is not released from all misery.

190. But who to the Buddha, Dhamma,
And Saṅgha* as refuge has gone,
Sees with full insight
The Four Noble Truths;*

191. Misery, the arising of misery,
And the transcending of misery,
The Noble Eightfold Path*
Leading to the allaying of misery.

192. This, indeed, is a refuge secure.
This is the highest refuge.
Having come to this refuge,
One is released from all misery.

193. Hard to come by is a person of nobility;
Not everywhere is he born.
Wherever that wise one is born,
That family prospers in happiness.

194. Joyful is the arising of Awakened Ones.
Joyful, the teaching of Dhamma true.
Joyful, too, the concord of the Saṅgha.
Joyful, the austere practice of those in concord.

195. Of one worshipping those worthy of worship,
Whether Awakened Ones or disciples,
Who have transcended preoccupying tendencies,*
Crossed over grief and lamentation,

196. Of one worshipping such as them,
Calmed ones who fear nothing,
The merit cannot be quantified
By anyone saying, 'It is of this extent.'

Chapter XV Happiness

197.   Ah, so pleasantly we live
Without enmity among those with enmity.
Among humans with enmity
Do we dwell without enmity.

198.   Ah, so pleasantly we live
Without affliction among the afflicted.
Among humans with affliction
Do we dwell without affliction.

199.   Ah, so pleasantly we live
Without restlessness among the restless.
Among humans who are restless
Do we dwell without restlessness.

200.   Ah, so pleasantly we live,
For whom there is nothing at all our own.
We shall become partakers of joy,
Even as the Radiant Devas.*

201.   Winning, one engenders enmity;
Miserably sleeps the defeated.
The one at peace sleeps pleasantly,
Having abandoned victory and defeat.

202.   There is no fire like passion,
No offence there is like ill will,
There is no misery like the *khandhas*,*
No ease there is higher than peace.

203.   Hunger is the illness most severe,
The *saṃkhāras* the greatest misery.
Knowing this as it is,
[One realizes] Nibbāna is ease supreme.

204.   Health is the highest gain,
             Contentment is the highest wealth,
             Those inspiring trust are kinsmen supreme,
             Nibbāna is ease supreme.

205.   Having tasted the flavour of seclusion
             And the flavour of calm,
             One is without distress, free from the bad,
             Drinking the flavour of the joys of dhamma.

206.   Good is the sight of noble ones,
             Their company is always pleasant.
             Without the sight of childish ones,
             One would constantly be at ease.

207.   One moving with childish ones
             Grieves for a long time.
             Misery is it to live with childish ones,
             As it always is with a foe.
             The wise one is one with whom to live is pleasant,
             As is a gathering of relations.
                Wherefore:

208.   The wise one, the insightful, and the learned,
             Having the virtue of enduring, dutiful, noble,
             A person true, intelligent,
             With such a one as this, one would associate,
             As the moon the path of the stars.

209.   One who exerts himself in what is not befitting
        And in the befitting exerts not,
        Having abandoned the beneficial, grasping for the dear,
        Envies the one who applies himself.

210.   Let one not be together with the dear,
        Nor ever with those that are not dear;
        Not to see the dear is misery,
        So too is it to see the non-dear.

211.   Therefore, let one not make endearment,
        For separation from the dear is bad.
        For whom there is neither the dear nor non-dear,
        For them are bonds not found.

212.   From the dear arises grief.
        From the dear arises fear.
        For one set free from endearment,
        There is no grief. Whence fear?

213.   From affection arises grief.
        From affection arises fear.
        For one set free from affection,
        There is no grief. Whence fear?

214.   From sensual attachment arises grief.
        From sensual attachment arises fear.
        For one set free from sensual attachment,
        There is no grief. Whence fear?

215.   From sensual desire arises grief.
        From sensual desire arises fear.
        For one set free from sensual desire,
        There is no grief. Whence fear?

216.   From craving arises grief.
        From craving arises fear.
        For one set free from craving,
        There is no grief. Whence fear?

217.   The one endowed with virtue and vision,
        Established in dhamma, speaking truth,
        That one, doing his own tasks,
        The folk hold dear.

218.   One in whom a wish for the Undefined* is born,
        Who would be clear in mind,
        Whose heart is not bound in sensual pleasures,
        Is called 'one whose stream is upward bound'.

219.   As when a person long absent
        Has come safely from afar,
        Relatives, friends, and well-wishers
        Greet with delight the one who has returned;

220.   Just so, one who has done wholesome deeds
        Has gone from this world to the beyond—
        The wholesome deeds receive such a one,
        Like relatives, a dear one who has returned.

Chapter XVII Wrath

221. Wrath one would leave behind,
     Measurement one would abandon, every fetter transcend.
     Who clings not to name and form,* and possesses nothing.
     Upon that one miseries do not fall.

222. Who can hold back arisen wrath,
     Like a swerving chariot,
     That one I call 'a charioteer',
     Any other one is merely a reins-holder.

223. With absence of wrath one would conquer the wrathful
        one;
     With good, one would conquer the bad one;
     With giving, one would conquer the stingy one;
     With truth, the one speaking falsehood.

224. Let one tell the truth, let one not be angry.
     Asked, let one give even when he has but little.
     By these three factors,
     One would go into the presence of the gods.

225. They who are gentle sages,
     Constantly restrained in body,
     Go to the Unshakeable Abode,*
     Whither having gone, they do not grieve.

226. Of those who always keep awake,
     Learning day and night,
     Upon Nibbāna intent,
     'Intoxicants' come to an end.

227. Of old this is, Atula,*
     It is not just of today:
     They find fault with one sitting silently;
     They find fault with one speaking much,
     And even with one speaking in moderation do they find
        fault.
     In [this] world there is no one not faulted.

228. There was not and will not be,
     And now there is not found,
     A person absolutely faulted,
     Or absolutely praised.

229. Whom the wise praise,
     Having observed day after day,
     That one of faultless conduct, intelligent,
     Of wisdom and virtue well composed—

230. Who is fit to fault that one,
     Who is like a coin of gold?
     Even the gods praise that one;
     One praised by Brahmā too.

231. Let one guard against physical intemperance;
     In body, let one be restrained.
     Having abandoned physical misconduct,
     In proper conduct with the body let one live.

232. Let one guard against intemperance of specch;
     In speech, let one be restrained.
     Having abandoned verbal misconduct,
     In proper conduct with speech let one live.

233. Let one guard against intemperance of mind;
     In mind, let one be restrained.
     Having abandoned mental misconduct,
     In proper conduct with the mind let one live.

234. Those restrained in body, wise,
     And also restrained in speech,
     Restrained in mind, wise,
     They indeed are perfectly restrained.

Chapter XVIII Stains

235.   Like a yellow leaf are you now;
       And even Yama's men* have appeared for you;
       And at the threshold of departure you stand;
       But even the journey's provisions you do not have.

236.   Make a lamp for yourself.
       Strive quickly! Become a wise one;
       With stains blown out, free of blemish,
       You shall go to the heavenly realm of the nobles.

237.   And you are now well advanced in age;
       You have started the journey to the presence of Yama.
       And, in between, there is not even a resting place for you;
       Even the journey's provisions you do not have.

238.   Make a lamp for yourself;
       Strive quickly! Become a wise one;
       With stains blown out, free of blemish,
       You shall not undergo birth and old age again.

239.   Gradually, would the wise one,
       Bit by bit, moment by moment,
       Blow out the stain that is one's own,
       Like a smith the stain of silver.

240.   As rust sprung from iron,
       Springing from that, eats that itself,
       So one's own actions lead
       One of unwise conduct to a state of woe.

241.   For chants [memorized], non-repetition is corrosive;
       For houses, non-maintenance is corrosive;
       Corrosive is sloth for physical appearance;
       For one who guards, heedlessness is corrosive.

242.   The stain of a woman is misconduct;
          To the giver, stinginess is the stain.
          Bad qualities indeed are stains,
          In this world and in that beyond.

243.   More staining than that stain
          Is ignorance, the worst of stains.
          Having abandoned this stain,
          Be you free of stains, O bhikkhus!

244.   Life is easily lived
          By a shameless one,
          A disparager, crafty as a crow,
          An obtruder, impudent and corrupt.

245.   But life is lived with hardship
          By one sensitive to shame, ever seeking purity,
          Free from clinging, and not impudent,
          Discerning, pure in the mode of life.

246.   Whoever in [this] world destroys life,
          And falsehood speaks,
          Takes what is not given,
          And goes to another's wife,

247.   And the man who engages in
          The drinking of intoxicants,
          Right here in this world
          He digs up his own root.

248.   Know this, dear fellow,
          Bad qualities are intemperate.
          Let not greed and the un-dhammalike way
          Oppress you into prolonged suffering.

249.   People give according to their faith,
          According as they are pleased.
          So, one who becomes sullen,
          About the food and drink of others [received],
          He does not gain integration,
          Be it by day or by night.

250. But the one in whom this is extirpated,
     Destroyed at its roots, abolished,
     He does gain integration,
     Be it by day or by night.

251. There is no fire like passion.
     There is no grip like ill will.
     There is no snare like delusion.
     There is no river like craving.

252. Easily seen is the fault of others,
     But one's own is hard to see.
     The faults of others
     He winnows like chaff;
     But conceals his own,
     As a shrewd gambler, the defeating throw.

253. Of one who sees the faults of others,
     Constantly holding ideas of disdain—
     His intoxicants increase;
     Far is he from the extinction of intoxicants.

254. In the sky there is no footstep;
     The recluse is not in externals;
     Enamoured with preoccupying tendencies* are the
          generations;
     Free of preoccupying tendencies are Tathāgatas.

255. In the sky there is no footstep;
     The recluse is not in externals;
     No *saṃkhāra* is eternal;
     There is no agitation among Buddhas.

Chapter XIX   The Firm in Dhamma

256.   Were one to settle a case capriciously,
One thereby does not become firm in dhamma.
But the one who would discriminate
Both what is and what is not the case—the sagacious
      one—

257.   Who leads others impartially
With dhamma, not capriciously,
The intelligent one, guarded by dhamma,
Is called 'one firm in dhamma'.

258.   One is not a learned one
Merely because one speaks much.
The one secure, without enmity, without fear,
Is called a 'learned one'.

259.   One is not a dhamma-bearer
Merely because one speaks much,
But who, having heard even a little,
Sees dhamma for himself,
And dhamma does not neglect,
He, indeed, is a dhamma-bearer.

260.   One does not become an Elder*
Because one's head is grey-haired;
Ripened his age,
'Grown old in vain' is he called.

261.   In whom there is truth and dhamma,
Harmlessness, restraint, control,
Who has the stains ejected, and is wise,
He indeed is called 'Elder'.

262.   Not because of speech-making
Or by attractiveness of appearance
Does one, envious, avaricious, deceitful,
Become a commendable man.

263. But in whom this is extirpated,
Destroyed at its roots, abolished,
He, having ill will ejected, wise,
Is called 'commendable'.

264. Not by a shaven head* is one a recluse,
If one lacks due observance, speaks untruth.
How can one possessed of longing and greed
Become a recluse?

265. But he who calms away the wrongs,
Great and small, in every way;
For having [so] calmed away the wrongs,
'A recluse' he is called.

266. Not for this is one a bhikkhu,
Merely that one begs of others;
Having taken up a gross dhamma,*
One is not thereby a bhikkhu.

267. Setting aside both merit and wrong
Who lives here the higher life,
Courses in the world discriminately,
He, indeed, is called 'bhikkhu'.

268. One does not become a sage by silence,
If confused and ignorant.
But a wise one, as if holding a set of scales,
Takes up the best,

269. And shuns wrongs, he is a sage;
For that reason he is a sage.
Who knows both in this world,
Is, for that, called a sage.

270. By harmlessness toward living beings
Is one called a Noble One.
One who is harmless toward all living beings
Is called 'noble one'.

271.   Not by precepts and rites,
         Nor again by much learning,
         Nor by acquisition of concentration,
         Nor by secluded lodging,

272.   Thinking 'I touched the ease of renunciation
         Not resorted to by ordinary people,'
         O bhikkhu, get not into contentedness,
         Not having attained extinction of intoxicants.*

Chapter XX The Path

273. Of paths, the eightfold* is the best.
      Of truths, the four statements.*
      Detachment is the best of dhammas.
      And of two-footed ones, the one endowed with eyes.*

274. Just this path, there is no other
      For purity of vision
      Do ye go along this [path];
      This is what will bewilder Māra.

275. Entered upon this,
      An end of misery you will make.
      Proclaimed indeed is the path by me,
      Having known the extrication of the arrows.*

276. By you is the task strenuously to be done;
      Tathāgatas* are proclaimers.
      Entered upon this path, the meditators
      Are released from the bond of Māra.

277. When through wisdom one perceives,
      'All samkhāras are transient,'*
      Then one is detached as to misery.
      This is the path of purity.

278. When through wisdom one perceives,
      'All samkhāras are suffering,'*
      Then one is detached as to misery.
      This is the path of purity.

279. When through wisdom one perceives,
      'All dhammas are without self,'*
      Then one is detached as to misery.
      This is the path of purity.

280.   Who is not exerting at the time for exertion,
        Young, strong, possessed of laziness,
        With mind filled with confused notions, indolent,
            lethargic—
        Does not find the way to wisdom.

281.   Watchful of speech, well restrained in mind,
        One would not do what is unwholesome by body too.
        These three modes of action one would purify.
        Let one fulfil the path made known by the sages.

282.   From meditativeness arises the great;
        From its absence, there is destruction of the great.
        Having known this twofold path for gain and loss
        Let one conduct oneself so that the great increases.

283.   Cut down the forest! Not a tree.
        From the forest, fear arises.
        Having cut down both forest and underbrush,
        O bhikkhus, be ye without forests.*

284.   Insofar as the underbrush is not cut away,
        Even to the smallest bit, of a man for women,
        Insofar is he one having [his] mind tethered,
        Like a suckling calf to its mother.

285.   Cut down affection for yourself,
        As with the hand, an autumn lily.
        Foster just the path to peace, Nibbāna,
        Taught by the One Who Has Travelled Well.

286.   'Here I shall dwell during the rains,*
        Here in winter and summer, too.'
        So the childish one thinks.
        He does not know of the danger.

287.   That man of entangled mind,
        Inebriated by sons and cattle,
        Death carries away
        Like a great flood, a sleeping village.

288.   No sons there are for protection,
        Neither father nor even relations,
        For one seized by the End-Maker;
        Among relations there is no protection.

289.   Knowing this fact,
        The wise one, restrained by virtue,
        Would make clear, right quickly,
        The path leading to Nibbāna.

Chapter XXI Miscellaneous

290. If by sacrificing a limited pleasure
   An extensive pleasure one would see,
   Let the wise one beholding extensive pleasure,
   A limited pleasure forsake.

291. Who wishes his own pleasure,
   By imposing misery on others,
   Who is contaminated by the contact of hate,
   He is not released from hate.

292. What is to be done, that is rejected.
   And what is not to be done, is done.
   Of those who are vain, heedless,
   The intoxicants increase.

293. But those who have well undertaken,
   Constantly, mindfulness with regard to body,*
   Persevering in what is to be done,
   They do not resort to what is not to be done.
   Of those mindful, attentive ones,
   The intoxicants come to an end.

294. Having slain mother and father*
   And two *khattiya* kings,*
   Having slain a kingdom* together with the subordinate,*
   Without trembling, the *brāhmaṇa* goes.

295. Having slain mother and father
   And two learned kings,*
   Having slain the tiger's domain, as fifth,*
   Without trembling, the *brāhmaṇa* goes.

296. Well awake* they arise, at all times,
   The disciples of Gotama,*
   In whom, both day and night,
   Constantly there is mindfulness on the Buddha.

297. Well awake they arise, at all times,
The disciples of Gotama,
In whom, both day and night,
Constantly there is mindfulness on Dhamma.

298. Well awake they arise, at all times,
The disciples of Gotama,
In whom, both day and night,
Constantly there is mindfulness on the Saṅgha.

299. Well awake they arise, at all times,
The disciples of Gotama,
In whom, both day and night,
Constantly there is mindfulness on the body.

300. Well awake they arise, at all times,
The disciples of Gotama,
In whom, both day and night,
The mind delights in harmlessness.

301. Well awake they arise, at all times,
The disciples of Gotama,
In whom, both day and night,
The mind delights in meditation.

302. Difficult it is to go forth, difficult to delight therein;
Difficult to live in are households—a suffering.
Suffering it is to live with uneven ones;
And travellers are trapped in suffering.
So, be not a traveller,*
And be not trapped in suffering.

303. The faithful one, endowed with virtue,
Possessed of fame and wealth,
To whatever region he resorts,
There, indeed, he is worshipped.

304. From afar the good ones are visible,
Like the snowy mountain.*
The bad ones here are not seen,
Like arrows shot in the night.

305.   Sitting alone, resting alone,
              Walking alone, unwearied,
              The one alone, who controls oneself,
              Would be delighted in the forest.*

306. The one who speaks lies, goes to hell,
     And the one who having done says, 'I don't do this.'
     Both of these, people of base deeds,
     Having passed away, become equal in the beyond.

307. Many having the yellow robe about their necks
     Are of bad qualities, uncontrolled.
     They, the bad ones,
     By bad deeds are led to hell.

308. Better that an iron ball be eaten,
     Glowing, like a flame of fire,
     Than that one should eat a country's alms food,*
     Being poor in virtue, lacking control.

309 Four conditions the heedless man comes by,
     Who resorts to the wives of others;
     Acquisition of demerit,
     Lack of agreeable sleep,
     Disgrace is third; hell is the fourth.

310. Acquisition of demerit
     And a lowly [future] course.
     And brief the delight of a frightened man with a
         frightened woman,
     The king too gives a heavy punishment—
     So let a man not resort to the wife of another.

311. Just as *kusa* grass,* wrongly grasped,
     Cuts the hand itself,
     So, reclusiveness wrongly handled,
     Drags one down to hell.

312. Whatever is a loose act,
     And what is a defiled observance—
     A 'higher life'* filled with suspicion—
     That is not of great fruit.

313.   If it is a thing to be done, let one do it,
        Let one advance decisively to it;
        For religious conduct that is slack
        Throws up dirt all the more.

314.   A misdeed is better not done;
        The misdeed torments hereafter.
        But a good deed is better done,
        Having done which, one does not regret.

315.   Like a border city
        Guarded both within and without,
        So, guard yourself.
        Let not the moment slip you by.
        Those for whom the moment is past
        Do indeed grieve, consigned to hell.

316.   They are ashamed of what is not shameful,
        They are not ashamed of what is shameful.
        Ones who endorse wrong views,*
        Such beings go to a state of woe.

317.   Those who see what is not fear as fear,
        And see no fear in fear,
        Ones who endorse wrong views,
        Such beings go to a state of woe.

318.   Those who regard what is not error as error,
        And see no error in error,
        Ones who endorse wrong views,
        Such beings go to a state of woe.

319.   But having known error as error,
        And non-error as non-error,
        Ones who endorse proper views,
        Such beings go to a state of weal.

Chapter XXIII The Elephant

320. Like an elephant in battle,
      The arrow shot from a bow,
      I shall endure the unwarranted word;
      The majority, indeed, are of poor virtue.

321. They take a tamed one to a crowd;
      On a tamed one a king mounts.
      Among humans a tamed one is best,
      One who endures the unwarranted word.

322. Excellent are tamed mules,
      Thoroughbreds and horses of Sindh,*
      Also tuskers, great elephants.
      But better than them is one who has subdued oneself.

323. Truly, not by these vehicles
      Could one go to a region unreached,
      As a tamed one goes
      By a well-subdued, disciplined self.

324. The tusker named Dhanapālaka,*
      Deep in rut, is hard to control.
      Bound, the tusker does not eat a morsel,
      But remembers the elephant forest.

325. When one is torpid and a big eater,
      A sleeper, who lies rolling about
      Like a great boar, nourished on grains—
      Being dull one enters the womb again and again.*

326. Formerly this mind set out awandering
      As it wished, where it liked, according to its pleasure.
      Today I will hold it back methodically
      Like one seizing a goad, an elephant in rut.

327.   Be delighters in awareness;
       Keep watch over your mind.
       Lift yourself up from the difficult road,
       Like a tusker, sunk in mire.

328.   Should one get a mature companion,
       Who will move about with one, a wise one who leads a
            good life,
       Let one move with him,
       All dangers overcoming, mindful and happy.

329.   Should one not get a mature companion,
       Who will move about with one, a wise one who leads a
            good life,
       Let one wander alone,
       Like a king who has left behind a conquered land,
       Like the elephant in the Mātaṅga forest.*

330.   A life of solitude is better;
       There is no companionship with the childish one.
       With little exertion, like the elephant in the Mātaṅga
            forest,
       Let one wander alone, and do no wrongs.

331.   When a need has arisen, friends are a blessing,
       A blessing is contentment with whatever [there be],
       A blessing is the wholesome deed at the end of life,
       A blessing it is to relinquish all sorrow.

332.   A blessing in the world is reverence for mother,
       A blessing, too, is reverence for father,
       A blessing in the world is reverence for the recluse,
       A blessing too reverence for the *brāhmaṇa*.

333.   A blessing is virtue into old age,
       A blessing is faith established,
       A blessing is the attainment of insight-wisdom,
       A blessing it is to refrain from doing wrongs.

Chapter XXIV Craving

334. The craving of a person who lives heedlessly
Grows like a *māluvā* creeper.*
He moves from beyond to beyond,
Like a monkey, in a forest, wishing for fruit.

335. Whomsoever in the world
This childish entangled craving overcomes,
His sorrows grow,
Like *bīraṇa* grass,* well rained upon.

336. But whosoever in the world
Overcomes this childish craving, hard to get beyond,
From him, sorrows fall away,
Like drops of water from a lotus leaf.

337. This I say to you. Good fortune to you [all],
As many as are here assembled.
Dig out the root of craving,
As one searching for *usīra** digs out *bīraṇa* grass.
Let not Māra break you again and again,
As a river, a reed.

338. As long as the roots are unharmed, firm,
A tree, though topped, grows yet again.
Just so, when the latent craving* is not rooted out,
This suffering arises again and again.

339. For whom the thirty-six streams,*
Flowing to what is pleasing, are mighty,
That one, whose view is debased,
The currents, which are thoughts settled on passion, carry
    away.

340. Streams* flow everywhere;
A creeper,* having burst upward, remains.
Having seen the creeper that has arisen,
Cut out with insight-wisdom its root.

341. Moved along and soaked by craving,
     Delights arise in a being.
     Those men who are bound to the agreeable, looking for
        pleasure,
     Do indeed go on to birth and old age.

342. Accompanied by craving,
     Folk crawl around like a trapped hare,
     Being held by fetters and bonds.
     They come by suffering again and again, for long.

343. Surrounded by craving,
     Folk crawl around like a trapped hare.
     Therefore, let a bhikkhu dispel craving,
     Wishing for his own detachment.

344. Who is free of the underbrush, but attached to the forest,*
     Who, set free from the forest, runs back to the forest;
     Come, see that person,
     Who, released, runs back to bondage itself.

345. That is not a strong bond, say the wise,
     Which is made of iron, of wood, or of [plaited] grass.
     Those excessively attached to jewels and ornaments
        [their attachment],
     And affection for sons and wives,

346. This is a strong bond, say the wise,
     Dragging down, lax [and yet] hard to loosen.
     Having cut off even this, they set out,
     Free of expectation, relinquishing sensual pleasures.

347. Those who are attached to passions fall back into the
        'stream',
     Like a spider, on a self-spun web.
     Having cut off even this, the wise proceed
     Free of expectation, relinquishing all suffering.

348. Let go in front, let go behind, let go in between!
     Gone to the further shore of existence,
     With mind released as to 'everything',
     You shall not again come upon birth and old age.

349. For a person having thoughts disturbed,
Acute of passion, looking for the pleasurable,
Craving increases all the more.
That one, indeed, makes the bondage firm.

350. But one who delights in allaying thoughts,
Who, ever-mindful, develops meditation on the
unpleasant,*
That one, indeed, will make an end,
That one will cut off Māra's bond.

351. The one who has arrived at the destination,
Free from fright, craving, and blemish,
Has broken the knives of existence.*
This is the final bodily form.

352. Without craving, free from grasping,
Skilled in terms of expression,
Who would know the combination of letters, what
precedes and what follows,
He, indeed, is called one having the last physical form,
Great person of great wisdom.

353. Conqueror of all, knower of all am I;
Untainted with regard to all dhammas.
Abandoning everything, released at the dissolution of
craving,
Having comprehended by myself, whom shall I point
out?

354. The gift of dhamma prevails over every gift,
The flavour of dhamma prevails over every flavour,
The delight in dhamma prevails over every delight,
The dissolution of craving subdues all suffering.

355. Possessions strike down one deficient in wisdom,
But not those seeking the beyond.
Through craving for possessions, one deficient in wisdom
Strikes himself down as one would the others.

356.   For fields, grasses are the bane,
              For humankind, sensual attraction is the bane.
              Hence, to those free from sensual attraction
              What is given yields much fruit.

357.   For fields, grasses are the bane,
              For humankind, ill will is the bane.
              Hence, to those free from ill will
              What is given yields much fruit.

358.   For fields, grasses are the bane,
              For humankind, confusion is the bane.
              Hence, to those free from confusion
              What is given yields much fruit.

359.   For fields, grasses are the bane,
              For humankind, longing is the bane.
              Hence, to those free from longing
              What is given yields much fruit.

360. Restraint with the eye is commendable,
Commendable is restraint with the ear.
Restraint with the nose is commendable,
Commendable is restraint with the tongue.

361. Restraint with the body is commendable,
Commendable is restraint with speech.
Restraint with the mind is commendable,
Commendable is restraint in all [the senses].
The bhikkhu who is restrained in all [the senses],
Is freed from all suffering.

362. The one restrained in hand, restrained in foot,
Restrained in speech, the one of best restraint,
Having delight in introspection, composed, solitary,
    contented—
That one they call a bhikkhu.

363. A bhikkhu, restrained in speech,
Who speaks in moderation, who is not haughty,
Who illustrates the meaning and the message,
Sweet is his speech.

364. Abiding in dhamma, delighting in dhamma,
Reflecting on dhamma, remembering dhamma,
A bhikkhu, does not fall away
From dhamma true.

365. Let one not treat what one has received with scorn,
Let one not live envying others.
A bhikkhu who is envying others
Does not come to integration [of mind].

366. If though a bhikkhu has received but little,
He does not treat his receipt with scorn,
Him, indeed, the gods praise,
Who is living purely, unwearied.

367.   For whom there is no 'sense of mine'
        Toward all that is name-and-form, in every way,
        Who does not grieve because of what is not;
        He, indeed, is called a bhikkhu.

368.   A bhikkhu dwelling in loving-kindness,
        Who is pleased in the Buddha's instruction,
        Would attain the state that is peace,
        The pacification of the *saṃkhāras*, bliss.

369.   O bhikkhu, bail out this boat.
        Bailed out, it shall go quickly for you.
        Having cut away both lust and hate,
        You shall then reach Nibbāna.

370.   Let one cut away the five, relinquish the five,*
        And, especially, cultivate the five.*
        A bhikkhu who has gone beyond five attachments
        Is called 'One who has crossed the flood'.

371.   Meditate, O bhikkhu, and be not heedless.
        Let not your mind whirl in the strand of sensuality.
        Do not swallow a metal ball, being heedless,*
        While burning; do not lament, 'This is woe.'

372.   There is no meditative absorption for one who lacks
                insight;
        There is no insight for one who is not meditating.
        In whom there is meditative absorption and insight,
        Truly, he is in Nibbāna's presence.

373.   For a bhikkhu who has entered an empty house,*
        Whose mind is at peace,
        Who perceives dhamma fully,
        There is delight unlike that of mortals.

374.   Howsoever one thoroughly knows
        The rise and demise of the *khandhas*,*
        One attains joy and delight
        That is ambrosia for those who are discerning.

375. Here, this is the first thing for a bhikkhu of insight:
Guarding the sense faculties, contentment,
And restraint in the *pātimokkha*.*
Associate with good friends
Who are living purely, unwearied.

376. Let one be in the habit of friendly relations,
Of competent conduct let one be.
Being of abundant joy thereby,
One shall make an end of suffering.

377. As the jasmine
Sheds its withered flowers,
So, O bhikkhu,
Shed sensual attachment and hatred.

378. A bhikkhu, with body pacified, speech pacified,
Who is possessed of peace, well composed,
Who has thrown out the world's material things,
Is called the 'one at peace'.

379. You yourself reprove yourself,
You yourself set yourself in order.
As a bhikkhu who is self-guarded, aware,
You shall dwell at ease.

380. Oneself, indeed, is patron of oneself,
Oneself is one's own guide.
Therefore, restrain yourself,
As a merchant, a noble steed.*

381. A bhikkhu, of abundant joy,
Pleased in the Buddha's instruction,
Would attain the state of peace,
The blissful alleviation of the *samkhāras*.

382. Truly, a young bhikkhu
Who engages in the Buddha's instruction
This world illumines,
Like the moon set free from a cloud.

Chapter XXVI The Brāhmaṇa

383. Having striven, cut off the stream!*
     Dispel sensualities, O *brāhmaṇa*,
     Having known the dissolution of the *saṃkhāras*,
     A knower of the Unmade* are you, O *brāhmaṇa*.

384. When, with regard to two dhammas,*
     A *brāhmaṇa* has reached the further shore,
     Then of that knowing one
     All fetters come to an end.

385. For whom the further shore or the nearer shore
     Or both do not exist,
     Who is free of distress, unyoked,
     That one I call a *brāhmaṇa*.

386. The one meditating, free of dirt, quietly sitting,
     Tasks done, free of intoxicants,
     Who has obtained the goal supreme,
     That one I call a *brāhmaṇa*.

387. By day glows the sun,
     At night shines the moon,
     In war-array the monarch glows.
     Meditating, a *brāhmaṇa* glows.
     But all day and night
     The Buddha glows in splendour.

388. As 'one who has banished wrong' is one a *brāhmaṇa*;*
     Because of 'living in calm' is one called a *samaṇa*.*
     Dispelling one's own stain
     —Therefore is one called 'gone forth.'

389. A *brāhmana* would not attack a *brāhmaṇa*,
     Or let loose [wrath] upon him.
     Shame on one who strikes a *brāhmaṇa*,
     And greater shame [on one] who lets loose [wrath] upon
        him.

390. When there is exclusion from what is pleasant to the
       mind;
     That is no little good for the *brāhmaṇa*—
     Whenever the intent to harm does cease,
     Then indeed is sorrow calmed.*

391. Of whom there is nothing ill done
     With body, with speech, with mind,
     Who is restrained in these three bases,
     That one I call a *brāhmaṇa*.

392. From whom one would learn dhamma
     Taught by the Fully Enlightened One,
     Let one pay homage to that one
     As a *brāhmaṇa* to the sacrificial fire.

393. Not by matted hair, nor by clan,
     Nor by birth does one become a *brāhmaṇa*.
     In whom is truth and dhamma,
     He is the pure one, and he is the *brāhmaṇa*.

394. What's the use of your matted hair, O you of poor
       insight?
     What's the use of your deerskin garment?*
     Within you is the jungle;
     The exterior you groom.

395. One who wears rags from a dust heap,*
     Lean, having veins [visibly] spread over body,
     Meditating alone in the forest,
     That one I call a *brāhmaṇa*.

396. And I do not call one a *brāhmaṇa*
     Merely by being born from a [*brāhmaṇa*] womb,
     Sprung from a [*brāhmaṇa*] mother.
     He is merely a '*bho*-sayer'*
     If he is a possessor of things.
     One who has nothing and takes nothing,
     That one I call a *brāhmaṇa*.

397.   Who does not tremble,
       Having cut off every fetter,
       Who has gone beyond attachments, unbound,
       That one I call a *brāhmaṇa*.

398.   Having cut off the strap and thong,
       Cord, together with the bridle,
       Who has lifted the bar,* awakened,
       That one I call a *brāhmaṇa*.

399.   Who unangered endures
       Insult, assault, and binding,
       Whose strength is forbearance, who has an army's
           strength,
       That one I call a *brāhmaṇa*.

400.   Who is free of anger, who observes the duties,
       Who is virtuous, free of the flow [of craving],
       Controlled, and in the final body,
       That one I call a *brāhmaṇa*.

401.   Like water on a lotus petal,
       Like a mustard seed on the point of an awl,*
       Who is not smeared with sensualities,
       That one I call a *brāhmaṇa*.

402.   Who comes to understand, even here,
       The destruction of sorrow,
       Who has put aside the burden, who is free of the bonds,
       That one I call a *brāhmaṇa*.

403.   One having profound insight, wise,
       Proficient as to path and non-path,
       Who has attained the highest goal,
       That one I call a *brāhmaṇa*.

404.   One who is not gregarious
       With both householders and homeless ones,*
       Living without an abode, desiring but little,
       That one I call a *brāhmaṇa*.

405. Having laid down the rod
      With regard to beings, the frightful and the firm,
      Who neither slays nor causes to slay—
      That one I call a *brāhmaṇa*.

406. One who is not opposing among those opposing,
      Who is calmed among those who have taken weapons,
      Free of grasping among those who are grasping,
      That one I call a *brāhmaṇa*.

407. From whom passion and ill will,
      Conceit and ingratitude, have been shed,
      Like a mustard seed from the tip of an awl,
      That one I call a *brāhmaṇa*.

408. Who would speak speech that is true,
      That is instructive and not harsh,
      By which one would anger none—
      That one I call a *brāhmaṇa*.

409. Who, here in this world, does not take what is not given,
      Whether long or short, small or great,
      Pleasant or unpleasant,
      That one I call a *brāhmaṇa*.

410. In whom are not found longings
      For this world and for the beyond,
      Without longing, released,
      That one I call a *brāhmaṇa*.

411. In whom are not found attachments,
      Who is without doubts due to understanding,
      Who has attained the plunge into the Deathless,
      That one I call a *brāhmaṇa*.

412. Who, here, has moved beyond attachment,
      Both the meritorious and the detrimental,
      Who is free of sorrow, free of dust, pure,
      That one I call a *brāhmaṇa*.

413. Who, like the moon, is spotless, pure,
Serene, unagitated,
In whom is extinct the desire for existence,
That one I call a *brāhmaṇa*.

414. Who has passed over this [muddy] path, this fortress,
Delusion, which is *saṃsāra*,
Who has crossed over it, gone beyond it, a meditator,
Passionless, without doubts,
Without grasping, pacified,
That one I call a *brāhmaṇa*.

415. Who, here, having renounced lusts,
Would go forth, a homeless one,
In whom is extinct sensual lust and [desire for] existence,
That one I call a *brāhmaṇa*.

416. Who, here, having renounced craving,
Would go forth, a homeless one,
In whom is extinct craving and [desire for] existence,
That one I call a *brāhmaṇa*.

417. Who, having abandoned the human bond,
Has transcended the heavenly bond,*
Who is released from all bonds,
That one I call a *brāhmaṇa*.

418. Who, having abandoned attachment and aversion,
Who has become cool,* free from substrates,*
A hero overcoming the entire world—
That one I call a *brāhmaṇa*.

419. Who knows in every way
The passing away and rebirth of beings,
Unattached, well gone, awakened,
That one I call a *brāhmaṇa*.

420. Whose course
Gods, *gandhabbas*,* and humans do not know,
Whose intoxicants are extinct, an Arahant,
That one I call a *brāhmaṇa*.

421. For whom there is nothing
     In front, behind, and in between,
     The one, without anything, ungrasping,
     That one I call a *brāhmaṇa*.

422. A bull,* splendid, heroic,
     A great sage, a victor,
     Passionless, who has bathed,* awakened,
     That one I call a *brāhmaṇa*.

423. One who knows [his] former lives,
     And sees the heavens and the states of woe,
     And who has reached the extinction of births,
     Who has perfected higher knowledge,
     Sage, who has fulfilled the final perfection,
     That one I call a *brāhmaṇa*.

EXPLANATORY NOTES

3   *perception . . . mental states*: the pure event of seeing, hearing, smelling, etc. an object is 'perception'; the concurrent rise of attachment, hate, anger, desire, etc. with regard to it is the mental states.

    polluted: that is, with mental states such as anger.

4   *Māra*: Māra stands for all that is antithetical to the religious enterprise. Variously represented as an evil being of great power out to wreck the religious life of persons, as the defiling forces of the psyche, the five aggregates of which the psycho-physical personality is made up (see note to p. 29), the influences of past karma, and, somewhat differently, Death itself. Also called King of Death (v. 46), End-Maker (v. 48), etc.

    defilements: unwholesome psychological qualities that vitiate the mind, all of which spring from the three 'roots' of (1) greed/craving/attachment, (2) hate/ill will/revulsion, and (3) ignorance/delusion/unawareness.

    yellow robe: the dress of the monk, symbolic of renunciation of worldly pursuits.

    passion: greed and all expressions of sensual desire. It is the first of the three unwholesome 'roots'.

5   *state of woe*: a state or world that is full of suffering. There are four such states mentioned: animal world, ghost world, world of the demonic Asuras, and the hell worlds.

    state of weal: a happy state of existence, i.e. the various heavenly worlds. Many classes of heavenly existence are mentioned, varying in degree of refinement of physical condition and happiness. But beings of such worlds are also subject to birth, decay, and death (except the Suddhāvāsā whose denizens attain liberation and are freed from the cycle of birth, death, and rebirth in that state itself).

    dhamma: a word rich in many different meanings. Here the Buddha's teaching and the way of living that is consonant with it.

6   *the Deathless*: Nibbāna.

    awareness: constantly occurring mindfulness, the supreme method commended by the Buddha for liberation from the ills of mind which are the root cause of suffering.

    noble ones: those who are on the path of liberation; who have attained any one of its four stages: Stream Winner, Once-Returner, Non-Returner, and Arahant, which last includes the Buddhas.

Nibbāna: (Skt. *Nirvāṇa*), the final goal of the Buddhist religious quest. It is psychologically represented as the extinction of greed, hate, and delusion, supreme happiness, etc., and metaphysically as Immortal, Undecaying, Unmade, Unconditioned, etc.

7 *Maghavan*: appellative of Sakka, chief God of two heavenly worlds, represented as an ardent admirer and supporter of the Buddha and his dispensation. The reference here is to an incident in which he got the better of his adversaries, the Asuras, by refraining from taking liquor and thus maintaining an aware, unintoxicated mind. His more frequent appellative, Inda, shows that he is the Buddhist form of the volatile and voluptuous Vedic Indra, god of lavishness and war and bringer of storms and rain.

bhikkhu: literally one who begs (for alms), that is, a mendicant monk. At the time of the Buddha, it was customary for members of religious orders to live on alms provided by the lay society, who regarded it as a duty to support the religious.

fetter: a mental state that binds beings to the wheel of birth, death, and rebirth. Ten such fetters are mentioned: (1) belief in a permanent personality, (2) sceptical doubt, (3) attachment to rules and rituals, (4) sensual craving, (5) ill will, (6) craving for birth in fine material heavens, (7) craving for supra-material heavens, (8) conceit, (9) restlessness and (10) psychological ignorance or delusion.

8 *The wholesome and the detrimental*: ten kinds of good deeds and ten kinds of bad are mentioned. The ten detrimental or unwholesome deeds are (*a*) *physical*: (1) killing, (2) stealing, (3) sensual misconduct; (*b*) *verbal*: (4) lying, (5) slander, (6) harsh speech, (7) frivolous speech; and (*c*) *mental*: (8) covetousness, (9) malevolence, and (10) wrong views. Abstaining from these physical, verbal, and mental unwholesome activities constitutes the ten good or wholesome deeds.

10 *Yama*: see note to p. 43.

learner: one who is undergoing the threefold training, namely in the higher ethical life, the higher mental concentration, and the higher insight. The first three Noble Ones are learners; the fourth has 'transcended the learning process' (see note to p. 6).

King of Death: see note to p. 4).

End-Maker: see note to p. 4).

12 *Fully Awakened One*: the Buddha, because he has awakened to the realities of all existence. (The word Buddha itself means the Awakened.)

13 *saṃsāra*: in almost all Indian religious traditions there is the belief in a cycle of birth, death, and rebirth, exit or transcendence from which is liberation, the final aim of the religious quest. The cycle is called *saṃsāra*.

13 *self*: the Buddhist teaching does not acknowledge the existence of an unchanging spiritual essence or self/soul in or behind consciousness (the mind in its most inclusive sense). This teaching of no-self or *anatta* is a specific characteristic of the Buddhist teaching.

self: in this context the word is used in the general sense of mind or mental condition. The fact that the word *self* is used in this sense and in the other sense mentioned in the above note is not to be taken as a contradiction.

deed ... of bitter fruit: the reference is to the teaching of kamma (Skt. karma). Deeds intentionally done affect the consciousness, condition the mind, and thereby, and in other ways, bring about their own result or 'fruit'.

14 *matured*: kamma may bring about its 'fruit' either immediately or after a lapse of (short or long) time. It brings its 'fruit' when 'matured'.

eat food with a kusa grass blade: that is, in minute quantity as an act of austere asceticism. (The *kusa* was one of the sacred grasses used in Indian ritual observances; it has a conspicuously narrow blade.) The idea is that such asceticism is nothing when compared with the understanding of dhamma and the attendant insight.

those who have gone forth: the monks who have renounced lay life and gone forth to live the life of a religious without any fixed abode. It was much later in time that monks began to live uninterruptedly in permanent monasteries.

15 *disengagement*: freedom from attachment.

17 *'let go'*: the same idea as in 'disengagement'.

A son: in India only the male offspring were qualified to perform religious rites for the benefit of departed parents and ancestors. Obtaining a son was therefore exceptionally treasured.

reach the shore beyond: transcend *saṃsāra*, attain liberation (see note to p. 13 above).

shadowy dhamma: a way of life entailing physical, verbal, and mental misconduct.

who has nothing: who has no obstacles to the religious life in the form of physical or psychological encumbrances/attachments.

factors of enlightenment: they are seven: mindfulness, investigation of dhamma, energy, rapture, tranquillity, concentration or integration of mind, and equanimity.

intoxicants: mental taints or biases brought about by sensual desire, desire for becoming or continued existence, and desire resulting from unawareness or psychological ignorance. A fourth that is often mentioned is the intoxication of views.

18   *gone the distance*: fulfilled the religious life.

    Fever: mental suffering.

    abode: metaphorical for attachment.

    hoarding: accumulation of things that make for creature comforts and the psychological accumulation of biases, etc.

    food: the Buddha frequently advised people not to over-indulge in, nor be attached to, food.

    pasture: the metaphor is probably to indicate that there is a certain 'space' in which they are happy

    freedom . . . empty, that has no sign: Nibbāna is 'empty' of greed, hate, and ignorance; these three are also not its signs (see note to p. 6).

    influxes: same as intoxicants (see note to p. 17).

    sustenance: see note to p. 18 regarding food.

    self-estimation: the Pāli word is *mana* which literally means 'measuring'. It is usually translated as conceit. One can have a high or low estimation or an estimation of equality: *mana* includes all of them.

19   *no faith*: the Commentary explains that where there is realization, the matter of faith is put aside. Normally, however, faith is regarded as the seed that grows into fully-fledged religious living.

    ungrateful: the original Pāli word if analysed as *a-kataññū* means 'ungrateful'; analysed as *akataṃ-ñū*, it will mean 'who knows the uncreated', that is, Nibbāna.

    burglar: the Pāli word literally means 'breaker of joints'. A joint may be where two walls meet: a burglar will break into a house here. It can also mean that which joins one to the wheel of existence and sorrow. To break this is to be fully liberated.

    opportunities: for continuing in the whirl of birth, death, and rebirth.

    ejected wish: when what has to be done is done, there is no need for entertaining future wishes or hopes.

    Who . . . supreme: this stanza purposely uses words that would normally be unexpected and even disturbing. It seems to have been meant to prod the listener/reader to look for the not-so-obvious deeper meanings, which describe the liberated person.

    Arahants: persons who have become 'worthy' (the literal meaning) by attaining liberation. As the first liberated, the Buddha is also an Arahant, but the word is commonly used to designate his disciples who were liberated by his Dhamma. In this context, both are meant. See also 'noble ones' at note to p. 6.

20   *gandhabba*: (Skt. *gandharva*) a class of semi-divine beings mentioned in Indian mythology.

20 *Brahmā*: in the celestial hierarchy, the Brahmas stand at the top. Brahmā in the singular refers to the divine being whom the Brahmins of the Buddha's time regarded as the Creator or Emanator of the worlds.

sacrifice: refers to the ritualistic offerings the Vedic Brahmins used to make to the gods.

21 *tend a fire*: refers to the fire worship of the Brahmins. Not only did they offer sacrifices to gods in the fire, but also it was expected that a Brahmin would keep a special sacrificial hearth lit in his home perpetually.

merit: the religious credit that would translate into future happiness or birth in a desirable status of life in the future.

virtue: moral conduct or ethical living (*sīla*).

insight: penetrative wisdom (*paññā*) that brings liberation. The three, *sīla*, *samādhi*, and *paññā*, referred to in vv. 110 and 111 constitute the three aspects of the path of liberation.

'the rise and demise': it is a cardinal feature of Buddhist teaching that whatever comes into being by the causal process inevitably disintegrates. This is a fact of life which one must necessarily understand.

immortal state: Nibbāna. See note to p. 6.

23 *the detrimental*: what is morally unwholesome. See note to p. 8.

matured: see note to p. 14.

24 *rich merchant with small caravan*: references to trading caravans abound in Buddhist literature. Merchants used to carry goods in fleets of carts, often across deserts and forests. Because such trips were fraught with hazards, especially with a small caravan, a merchant would try to take the safest route.

If on the other hand . . . not doing it: this is a rather strange verse. According to the Commentary 'one not doing it' should mean one who does something without a bad intention. The bad intention is like the wound in the hand.

That spot in the world . . . overwhelm one: these two verses are also unusual, not fully consonant with the classical Theravāda teaching about kamma. According to that teaching one is not inevitably bound by past kamma. A person who realizes the harm that may come from bad deeds can do much to mollify the effects of kamma.

26 *wandering about naked*: refers to ascetics who eschewed clothing in hope of discarding yet another worldly possession.

matted hair: some followers of austere asceticism would not wash, cut, or otherwise neaten their hair. The hair would just grow into tangled knots.

brāhmaṇa: Skt./Pāli form of Brahmin. In the caste hierarchy of Hindus, Brahmins stood at the top and were the only persons entitled to officiate in religious ceremonies. But one had to be born a Brahmin, there was no way to become one. The Buddha discarded these traditional notions and often used the word in an idealistic sense to mean the truly religious person.

27 *amenable ones*: the Commentary explains this as 'amenable to advice and instruction'.

28 *beautified image*: reference is to the body which we try to make attractive in various ways.

   gourds Discarded in autumn: reference seems to be to some variety of summer gourds that grew in such abundance that many were left unused and wasted away exposed to the elements in autumn.

   city: reference is to the body, as an assemblage of parts.

29 *I ran through saṃsāra . . . has it come*: these verses are traditionally regarded as ecstatic statements made by the Buddha after he attained Enlightenment.

   saṃkhāras: according to the Buddhist teaching the psycho-physical personality is made up of five aggregates. (1) physical form, (2) feelings, (3) perceptions, (4) dynamic and usually unconscious activities of the psyche, and (5) consciousness in a wide inclusive sense. *Saṃkhāras* are the fourth aggregate.

30 *watches*: the night was divided into three equal parts called the watches.

   māluvā creeper: the simile of the *māluvā* creeper spreading over a tree and bringing about its destruction is found at several places in the Buddhist Canon.

31 *detrimental view*: in the Noble Eightfold Path, the first is 'right view', or 'proper view', that is, the views commended in the teaching. Not to have such views is to be deficient in wisdom.

   Like the fruits of a reed: the Commentary says that banana, bamboo, and reed are plants of which the appearance of fruit signals the end of their life cycle.

32 *world-augmenter*: according to the Commentary 'world' here signifies *saṃsāra*. See note to p. 13.

33 *psychic power*: in most Indian religious systems reference is made to extra-sensory powers like the ability to read others' thoughts, see and hear what takes place in distant places, see events of future and past time, move through space, etc. as being obtained by feats of meditation and mental development.

   dhamma: means 'characteristic quality', of truthfulness in this context.

33   *Stream Attainment*: the first of four attainments on the path to liber-
     ation. With this Attainment the first three of the ten fetters are
     destroyed. (See notes to pp. 6 and 7.)

34   *pātimokkha*: summary of rules of the monastic discipline. All fully
     ordained monks and nuns were to recite this summary in assembly
     twice a month on the full moon and new moon days.

35   *Saṅgha*: the community of ordained monks and nuns. The term is
     also used to designate the totality of disciples who have attained any
     one of the four attainments of the Path (see notes to pp. 6, 7,
     and 33). In the latter case, a member of the Saṅgha need not neces-
     sarily be an ordained person. The Buddha, Dhamma, and the
     Saṅgha constitute the 'three jewels' and the 'three refuges' of
     Buddhists.

     Four Noble Truths: (1) the fact that there is inevitable suffering in life,
     (2) that suffering is the result of causes (which the Buddha has
     pointed out), (3) that it is possible to go beyond suffering and (4)
     that there is a path going beyond suffering—these are called the
     Four Noble Truths. The whole Buddhist teaching is based upon the
     recognition of these truths.

     The Noble Eightfold Path: the religious life recommended is called
     the Noble Eightfold Path. It consists of the following: right or
     proper view, thought, speech, activities, livelihood, effort, mindful-
     ness, and concentration. Following this path, one is enabled to put
     an end to suffering. The Eightfold Path constitutes the fourth of the
     Four Noble Truths. See also v. 273.

36   *preoccupying tendencies*: preoccupying tendencies or fantasies are
     the result ot the mind being caught up in the various moulds of
     attachment, traditionally given as craving, addiction to views, and
     egoistic measurement or self-estimation. When they are operating,
     the mind is not fully awake to immediate reality.

37   *Radiant Devas*: divine beings of a heavenly world whose denizens
     'feed on joy and live out their days solely in joy' and from whose
     bodies 'radiance issues like streaks of lightning from layers of
     cloud'.

     khandhas: the five aggregates (see, on *saṃkhāras*, note to p. 29).

40   *Undefined*: Nibbāna. So called because it is not possible to describe it
     with any attributes. See note to p. 6.

41   *name and form*: this term stands for the totality of physical (form)
     and mental (name) factors that make up the personality, that is, the
     five aggregates.

     Unshakeable Abode: another term for Nibbāna.

     Atula: the Commentary says this is the name of the person to whom this verse was addressed. The reader must remember that the *Dhammapada* consists of verses taken from here and there from the known canonical texts, as well as from other compatible sources.

43 *Yama's men*: in the Vedas, Yama is the king of the world of the dead. In the Buddhist texts he is represented in the same role. The appearance of *Yama's men* is an indication that Death is beckoning.

45 *preoccupying tendencies*: see note to p. 36.

46 *Elder*: a senior member of the Buddhist monastic order is called a *thera*. The word means an elder. This was how the orthodox doctrine prevalent in Kampuchea, Laos, Myanmar, Sri Lanka, and Thailand came to be called Theravāda, 'teaching of the Elders'.

47 *shaven head*: members of the Buddhist Saṅgha were required to shave their heads.

gross dhamma: there is probably a corruption of the text here. John Brough, in *The Gāndhārī Dharmapada* (London: Oxford University Press, 1962), 192, surmised that the text must originally have had a reading that gave the sense ' "a *dharma* no better than that of living in a house", i.e., a *dharma* concerned simply with obtaining enough food to live on'—therefore very different from the way of life recommended to Buddhist monks. Recently, K. R. Norman, in *The Word of the Doctrine (Dhammapada)* (Oxford: published by the Pali Text Society, 1997), 125–6, has shown that this is very plausible and suggested that 'the verse is a reference to brahmanical teaching about the householder, and to its incompatibility with being a *bhikkhu* in the Buddhist sense of the word'.

48 *extinction of intoxicants*: see note to p. 17. 'Intoxicants' are extinguished when one becomes an Arahant.

49 *paths . . . eightfold*: see note to p. 35.

four statements: the statements that designate the Four Noble Truths.

endowed with eyes: the Buddha, who has the Dhamma-eye of insight wisdom.

extrication of the arrows: in his wisdom, the Buddha has proclaimed the Path which draws out the arrows of greed, hate, and psychological ignorance.

Tathāgatas: literally, *tathāgata* means 'one who has gone thus'. Often it is translated as 'wayfarer'. The term refers to the Buddhas. Another similar epithet is *sugata*, 'the one who has gone or travelled well', as at v. 285.

saṃkhāras are transient: *saṃkhāras* in this context means all phenomena that have causally come into being, which are all evanescent and liable to disintegrate. This is the first of the three characteristic signs of conditioned phenomena.

49   *saṃkhāras are suffering*: the second characteristic sign of conditioned phenomena is that they are unsatisfactory in the final
analysis.

dhammas are without self: this is the third of the three characteristic
signs. But it is not as wide-embracing as the first two. It is restricted
to 'dhammas', that is, all aspects of consciousness. (See note to p.
3.) There is no unchanging self or soul in or behind the phenomena of consciousness.

50   *Cut down . . . forests*: this verse is somewhat similar to v. 97, though
not as cryptic. Here *forest and underbrush* is metaphorical for mental
defilements, large and small, as the Commentary explains.

the rains: the rainy season, the four lunar months between roughly
mid-August and the beginning of December. During this period of
monsoon rains, the monks, who originally rarely stayed for long
periods at one place, were required to spend time in a suitable chosen
locality.

52   *mindfulness with regard to body*: meditation or awareness of bodily
processes, one of the four mindfulness meditations. The other three
are mindfulness of feelings, of mind, and of mental objects. These
four meditations are described as the only way that leads to the
attainment of purity, the ending of pain and grief, and the realization of Nibbāna.

mother and father: craving and conceit, according to the
Commentary.

two khattiya kings: according to the Commentary, the two major
metaphysical concepts challenged by Buddhism are meant. They are
(1) the notion of eternal self and eternal matter and (2) the notion
that death is the end of everything. (The *khattiya*s were the ruling
caste; only a *khattiya* was usually considered qualified to become
king.) The metaphor of the king is employed because of the central-
ity of these two concepts in the spectrum of philosophical views that
were current during the time of the Buddha.

kingdom: the Commentary explains this as standing for the twelve
'bases' on which mental activity and consciousness depend. They are
eye and visual objects, ear and objects of hearing, nose and olfac-
tory objects, tongue and objects of taste, body and objects that can
be felt by touch, and mind and mental objects.

subordinate: the commentarial explanation is that this stands for
craving which depends upon the above twelve factors just as a king's
subordinate depends upon the king.

learned kings: kings of Brahmin descent. (The Pāli word translated
as 'learned' is *sotthiya*, which means a learned Brahmin.) This again
stands for the two extreme views of eternalism and annihilationism,
so the Commentary says.

the tiger's domain, as fifth: according to the Commentary reference is to a domain that is both a source of fear and difficult to traverse; a metaphorical representation of the five hindrances—desire for sensuality, ill will, sloth and torpor, agitation and remorse, and (sceptical) doubt—because they deflect virtuous qualities.

Well awake: going to sleep with mindfulness and rising up with mindfulness.

Gotama: (Skt. Gautama). The family name of Prince Siddhattha (Skt. Siddhārtha) who came to be known as the Buddha after Enlightenment.

53 *be not a traveller*: travel here is a metaphor for leading the ordinary worldly life.

snowy mountain: the Himalayas (from *hima*: snow).

54 *delighted in the forest*: the meditator would find delight in the seclusion of the forest and not the crowded life which is not helpful for contemplative pursuits.

55 *eat a country's alms food*: in the early period of the Buddhist monastic order, there was no cooking done at the monasteries. Monks subsisted on alms given by lay people. See notes to pp. 7 and 35.

kusa grass: see note to p. 14.

'higher life': religious life led for the sake of realizing Nibbāna.

56 *wrong views*: right or proper view, the first step of the Noble Eightfold Path, means the understanding of the Four Noble Truths. Any view not consonant with this would be a wrong view.

57 *horses of Sindh*: horses of Sindh (the region watered by the river *Sindhu* or *Indus*) were reputed for high trainability and general excellence.

Dhanapālaka: the Commentary mentions the story of an elephant Dhanapālaka who was caught for service of the king of Kāsi. The trainers, trying to domesticate it, gave it a richly appointed stable and excellent food. But it would have none of all this and thought only of its forest home and its mother who was in grief at being separated from her son.

enters the womb again and again: is subject to birth in *saṃsāra* again and again.

58 *elephant in the Mātaṅga forest*: the Commentary relates the story of Pārileyyaka, an elephant who tired of life in the herd and wandered alone and ministered to the Buddha, who was himself dissatisfied with the indiscipline of some monks and was staying alone in the same forest.

59 *māluvā creeper*: see note to p. 30.

59 *bīraṇa grass*: a grass said to grow luxuriantly during the rainy season.

usīra: the fragrant root of the *bīraṇa* grass.

latent craving: the ordinary individual's mind is beset with hidden proclivities or latent tendencies (*anusaya*) of sensuous greed, aggressiveness, sceptical doubt, conceit, and craving for continued existence. Freedom from suffering is possible only when they are completely eliminated.

thirty-six streams: the Commentary explains this as the *three* dimensions of craving (for sensuality, for continued existence, and for cessation of existence) flowing from the *twelve* 'bases'. See note to p. 52.

Streams: of craving mentioned in the previous verse, v. 339.

creeper: metaphorical for craving that has arisen.

60 *underbrush . . . forest*: see note to p. 50.

61 *meditation on the unpleasant*: contemplation of the body's impurity.

knives of existence: this may also be translated as 'arrows of becoming', that is, desires for continuity. Compare note to p. 49.

64 *cut away the five, relinquish the five*: reference to the ten fetters. See note to p. 7.

cultivate the five: the five 'faculties' of faith, enterprise, mindfulness, concentration, and insight-wisdom.

Do not swallow a metal ball, being heedless: being heedless of meditative awareness is like swallowing a metal ball heated in hell.

empty house: places of solitude are commended for meditation. Among them are empty houses, the foot of a tree, and cemeteries.

rise and demise of the khandhas: reference to the teaching that whatever comes into being by the causal process is liable to disintegrate. On *khandhas*, see notes to pp. 37 and 29.

65 *pātimokkha*: see note to p. 34.

a merchant, a noble steed: the Commentary explains: just as one who expects to get a profit from a good horse controls it and attends on it, bathing and feeding it three times a day.

66 *cut off the stream*: the stream of craving, according to the Commentary.

Unmade: Nibbāna.

two dhammas: the two kinds of meditation recommended in Buddhist teachings, tranquillity meditation and insight meditation, also called *samādhi* and *paññā*. The first aims at reaching one-pointedness and non-distraction of the mind, leading to the meditative states called the absorptions. The other aims at 'penetrative understanding by direct meditative experience, of the impermanency, unsatisfactoriness and impersonality of all phenomena' (Nyanatiloka, *Buddhist Dictionary: Manual of Buddhist Terms and Doctrines* (Colombo: Frewin & Co., Ltd., 3rd revised and enlarged edition, 1972), s.v. *samatha-vipassanā*).

banished wrong ... brāhmana: the text here resorts to a kind of etymologizing which cannot be brought out in an English translation—'banished wrong' in Pāli is *bāhita-pāpa*. Using the similarity in sound of *bāh-* and *brāh-*, it is assumed that the real meaning of the word *brāhmana* (a Brahmin) is *one who has banished wrong*.

living in calm   samana: similar to the immediately preceding note, the Pāli for 'living in calm' is *samacariyā*. This word then is assumed as conveying the true meaning of *samana* (a monk), on the strength of the common element *sama-*.

67 *A brāhmana would not attack ... sorrow calmed*: there is great uncertainty about the authenticity of the text of these verses, as shown by John Brough in *The Gāndhārī Dharmapada*, edited with an introduction and commentary (London: Oxford University Press, 1962), 180–3. But the author of the extant Pāli Commentary is not concerned with such problems. It is also quite likely that at his time, there was no awareness of any textual complexities in these verses. There was a received text and an accepted rendering and, as long as the rendering is consonant with the substance of Buddhist ethics, the commentators have no interest in raising questions about the text.

matted hair ... deerskin garment: traditional accoutrements of an ascetic. See also verse 141 and note to p. 26.

wears rags from a dust heap: monks of early times were evidently not always materially well supported. For this reason, and also from a sense of self-chosen austerity, some of them wore robes stitched from cloth discarded by lay people.

'bho-sayer': *bho* is a term added to the name of a person, indicative of the speaker's polite attitude toward that person. It was a custom that existed among Brahmins. In Buddhist texts, Brahmins as a rule address the Buddha as *'bho Gotama'*.

68 *strap ... thong ... Cord ... bridle ... bar*: according to the Commentary, these terms stand for hate, greed, wrong views, latent biases, and psychological ignorance.

water on a lotus petal ... a mustard seed on the point of an awl: neither would get attached to its base.

not gregarious With both householders and homeless ones: not 'contaminated' by intimacies with lay people or with other monks, according to the commentarial explanation.

70   *human bond ... heavenly bond*: craving for human and divine pleasures.

become cool: refers to the alleviation of the fever of lusts and hate with the attainment of Nibbāna.

free from substrates: the Pāli word for 'substrates' is *upādhi*, which expresses a variety of meanings: possessions and acquisitions (internal/external) to which one clings, as well as the process of clinging itself; constituents, experiences, and the causal ground of conditioned existence.

gandhabbas: see note to p. 20.

71   *bull*: words for majestic animals were often used in Pāli and Sanskrit in referring to great personages. The Commentary suggests the usage here is for indicating (inner) strength and imperturbability.

bathed: washed away defilements, according to the Commentary. The Pāli term used here, *nahātaka*, is the equivalent of Skt. *snātaka*, a word which is used to refer to a Brahmin who has finished his formal Vedic education and taken the ceremonial bath. The Buddha speaks of the value of an internal bath or purification.